Tallinn

Text by Steven Q. Roman
Photography by Anna Mockford and Nick Bonetti
Edited and designed by Roger Williams
Series Editor: Tony Halliday

D0993739

Berlitz POCKET GUIDE

Tallinn

First Edition (2005)
Reprinted 2006 (twice)

PHOTOGRAPHY CREDITS
Anna Mockford and Nick Bonetti 6, 9, 10, 12, 13, 22, 24, 26, 28, 29, 31, 32, 33, 34, 36, 38–9, 41, 42, 44, 47, 48, 49, 50, 53, 55, 56, 57, 59, 61, 62, 63, 64, 66, 67, 68, 69, 70, 73, 75, 76, 77, 79, 80, 83, 85, 87, 88, 89, 91, 92, 94, 97, 99; Topham Picturepoint 21
Cover picture by: Connie Coleman/Stone/ Getty Images

CONTACTING THE EDITORS
Every effort has been made to provide accurate information in this publication, but changes are inevitable. The publisher cannot be responsible for any resulting loss, inconvenience or injury. We would appreciate it if readers would call our attention to any errors or outdated information by contacting Berlitz Publishing, PO Box 7910, London SE1 1WE, England.
Fax: (44) 20 7403 0290;
e-mail: berlitz@apaguide.co.uk
www.berlitzpublishing.com

▶ Toompea Castle (page 30), from the 13th century onwards the historic seat of power in Estonia

Great architecture and a turbulent history characterise Dome Church (page 34), Tallinn's grand Lutheran cathedral ◀

A Toompea viewing platform (page 36) gives a fairytale view ▼

TOP TEN ATTRACTIONS

The Gothic Town Hall (page 41) has fine medieval woodcarvings among its treasures

The eye-catching clock of Holy Spirit Church (page 43) has been ticking since the 1600s

St Catherine's Passage (page 52), with its craft workshops and medieval ambience

The Aleksander Nevski Cathedral (page 28) with its three onion domes

A celebration of a country's rural roots: the Estonian Open Air Museum (page 66)

Once Tallinn's main marketplace, Town Hall Square (page 40) is still the life and soul of the Old Town

A reminder of imperial Russia: Peter the Great's Kadriorg Palace (page 58)

CONTENTS

INTRODUCTION

The secret is out – the world has finally woken up to this amazing little Baltic city that's steeped in history, pulsing with energy, easy to reach and, most of all, beaming with fairytale charm. In the few years since it re-emerged from Soviet-era isolation, Estonia's capital has become renowned for its fascinating Old Town, one of the most intact medieval town centres in Europe, and for the inspiring progress it has made in digging itself out from the rubble of the USSR and transforming itself into a modern metropolis. With all that Tallinn has going for it, the city is, not surprisingly, now one of the world's fastest-growing tourist destinations.

Nestled on the southern shore of the Gulf of Finland, this cosy city of just 400,000 inhabitants occupies an enviable position as a regional gateway. Its nearest neighbour, Helsinki, is only 90 minutes away by hydrofoil, and two of Northern Europe's most spectacular port cities, Stockholm and St Petersburg, can both be reached by overnight ferry. Latvia's capital, Riga, is a five-hour bus ride from Tallinn. With this location at the crossroads of East and West, and between Scandinavia and the Baltic states, Tallinn is increasingly used as a base for visitors exploring this corner of Europe, and has itself become an essential – and unforgettable – stop on any tour of the region.

Tallinn's role as a port-of-call between here and there is nothing new. In fact, that's been the city's defining feature since the early 13th century, when Danish troops and German crusaders invaded Estonia and laid the foundations of a major commercial hub. Soon after, Tallinn became a member of the Hanseatic League, an all-important associ-

St Catherine's Passage, Tallinn's most picturesque lane

ation of merchant cities during medieval times. It grew rich in the 14th and 15th centuries as the middleman in trade between the West and Novgorod in Russia. In the centuries that followed, the Swedish empire, the Russian empire and the Soviet Union each conquered this desirable port city, making their own intriguing contributions to Tallinn's urban landscape.

A Modern City in a Medieval Milieu

Without question, Tallinn's most valuable treasure is its Old Town – a remarkable survivor from the Middle Ages. Encircled by a centuries-old city wall, this is a beguiling place of narrow streets and intimate squares, ancient houses and towering church spires.

Like no other place in Europe, this area has somehow managed to hang on to its medieval atmosphere despite centuries of commerce, war and political change. The neighbourhood owes much of its survival to a series of historic accidents. Economic downturns kept construction in check, and at critical junctures, shrewd political settlements prevented the town from being sacked. The city's famous defensive wall, most of which is still intact, also helped a great deal in preserving the town for future generations. The area suffered from Soviet bombing towards the end of World War II, and from some dubious reconstruction that followed, but the ensuing occupation also had at least one unexpected benefit: trapped as it was in the amber of the Soviet Union, Tallinn's Old Town escaped

Tallinn is a popular destination for Finnish shoppers, particularly those after cheap deals on alcohol, which is heavily taxed in Finland. These shoppers had every reason to toast Estonia's accession to the EU in 2004, as they can now bring back unlimited amounts of booze.

Cycle taxis offer a novel way of touring the city

the over-development inflicted on similar cities in the West. Now for the most part restored to its original glory, the Old Town once again belongs to the world; in 1997, it was inscribed on UNESCO's list of world heritage sites.

But don't think of the Old Town as a static museum piece – it's nothing of the kind. This is the heart of Tallinn, the hub of its busy and eclectic restaurant scene and home to the city's famously raucous nightlife. Scattered amid the 15th-century buildings are trendy cafés, most of them offering wireless internet (WiFi) so that laptop-wielding locals can stay connected with the world. Town Hall Square, at the centre of the Old Town, is home to countless rock concerts, festivals and other performances. Bustling markets fill the streets, commingling with crowds of foreign visitors, all of whom add their own energy to the mix. And shopping here knows no limits. In short, as ironic as it sounds, the Old Town is where the heart of modern Tallinn beats the strongest.

This captivating part of town usually keeps visitors exploring for days, not because the area is large (in fact, intimacy is a major part of its appeal), but because there's always a new detail to see each time you meander through the same street. Even the most passive tourists are drawn to the Old Town; simply lounging in a terrace café and soaking up the unique 13th–16th-century ambience is just as good a way to enjoy Tallinn as trekking through it, guidebook in hand, making sure you leave no cobblestone unturned.

As much as there is to see in the Old Town, limiting yourself to this area would be a crime. Within the city limits you can see the spectacular Kadriorg Palace, built for Russian Tsar Peter the Great, the beautiful Pirita beach and river area, the fascinating ruins of the 15th-century St Bridget's Convent, the re-created farm villages in the Rocca al Mare Open Air Museum and some rather curious, Soviet-era construc-

Internet access in one of Europe's most hi-tech cities

tions on the outskirts of town. Also, a number of relatively undiscovered cities not far from Tallinn offer fantastic day-trip opportunities, and shouldn't be passed up.

People and Economy

Don't call it Eastern Europe. While the term might fit geographically, Estonia sees itself as having much more in common with Nordic countries than with its Slavic, or even Baltic neighbours. Indeed, the country's language and ethnic roots are Finno-Ugric, closely related to their cousins, the Finns. Maybe it's not surprising then that Estonians, like the Scandinavians and the Finns, tend to be serious, hard-working people, with a somewhat stoic manner. They're less gregarious and less likely to laugh than Spanish or Italians, but it doesn't mean they don't get the joke.

> Tallinn is one the most hi-tech cities in Europe, and the country has been dubbed E-stonia. As well as the ubiquitous wireless internet (WiFi) and the most advanced ID cards, the city has systems to pay for car parking and bar bills by text messaging from mobile phones.

They're also a people whose desire for self-determination runs deep. Perhaps that's why, after regaining independence in 1991, they were so quick to dust off a half-century of Soviet grey and rapidly catch up, economically and culturally, to the rest of Europe. Thanks to tough economic policies and liberal investment laws, Estonia has outstripped all other former Soviet states – and several Eastern European ones – in its recent development. Surpassing all expectations, it joined the European Union in 2004.

In the streets of Tallinn, this economic boom is clearly visible. The downtown area adjacent to the Old Town is developing at a breakneck pace, with Soviet eyesores being replaced by gleaming shopping malls and high-rise hotels. People are well dressed, offices are immaculate, and everyone over the age of five seems to be talking on a mobile phone. Indeed Estonians' love of all things high-tech has become something of a cliché, with '@' road signs pointing to internet access points and nearly all drivers paying for parking via SMS text message.

For the visitor, all this adds up to a more convenient, comfortable stay. Western attitudes towards service are the norm, the English language is nearly universal in the town centre, while hotels and even some restaurants can be booked online, and credit cards are accepted almost everywhere.

Seasons

Tallinn's extreme climate means that it's a highly seasonal city, as far as tourism – or anything else – goes. During the short period of warm weather, usually May to August, flocks of cruise-ship passengers and other visitors descend on the Old Town, filling the restaurants and hotel rooms. Still, this is the best time to visit, with the weather at its friendliest, festivals and concerts easiest to find, and the city generally at its most vibrant. That said, a visit in the off-season is perfectly reasonable for anyone who wants to avoid the crowds. There will still be plenty to see and do, even when outdoor cafés are no longer an option, and you'll have the enchanting medieval streets almost to yourself. A visit during winter, provided you're dressed properly for it, can be a truly magical experience as the snow blankets the tiled rooftops and the town turns on its Christmas charm.

Vernacular style at the Estonian Open Air Museum

A BRIEF HISTORY

A quick glance at Tallinn's history will leave no doubt as to why locals are so fiercely passionate about their independence. For nearly all of the past eight centuries their nation has been ruled by one foreign power after another, starting with subjugation by the Danish crown, then German crusaders, the Swedish empire, the Russian empire and, most recently, the Soviet Union. It's fairly remarkable that, against these odds, the Estonians have been able to hang on to their language and cultural identity through the years.

The secret to their resilience might be that their roots run incredibly deep. While historians argue about just exactly when the ancestors of the ancient Eesti (or 'Aestii' as the Romans called them) arrived on the Baltic coast, most put the date some time between 8000 and 3000BC.

Little is known about the pre-Christian period of Estonia's history, but archaeological evidence suggests that in the years before the arrival of the first invaders, the northern Estonian Rävala people lived a clan-like existence, engaged in farming, fishing and, increasingly, trade with their Baltic

A city steeped in history

Sea neighbours. By the 12th century AD, they had built a wooden fortress on Toompea hill, which the Arab cartographer Abu Abdallah Muhammed al-Idrisi marked on his world map in 1154 as a 'seasonal stronghold'. This was the first mention of Tallinn, or at least its precursor, in historical records.

First Invaders

In the early 13th century, the Pope's call for a crusade against the pagan peoples around the Baltic Sea prompted a bloody and complicated struggle between Swedes, Danes, Russians, German crusaders and local tribes. As part of this land grab, King Valdemar II of Denmark conquered the Estonians' stronghold on Toompea in 1219, immediately replacing it with his own fortress and subjugating northern Estonia. Valdemar's victory was a key turning point in

The Danes take Tallinn, 1219

Estonia's history, marking the beginning of a long period of foreign rule, with Toompea, the hill at the centre of Tallinn, always the regional seat of power.

German crusaders had meantime gained a foothold in Riga and were battling their way northward. In 1227, their military arm, the Order of the Brothers of the Sword, occupied Toompea and gained control of the Danish holdings. A papal decree returned power to the Danes in 1238, by which time a feudal system, with Germans as landlords, had been instituted in the country-

When Tallinn city was enclosed by a wall, it did not include Toompea, home to the Baltic German nobility and base for Estonia's foreign rulers. Tension between the two was fuelled by a city law that allowed any runaway peasant who managed to stay within the town walls for a year and a day to be declared free of his master, providing the city with much-needed labour. Tallinn and Toompea remained separate, and often at odds, until they were united in the late 1880s.

tryside. More significantly for the development of Tallinn, the Order had invited 200 German merchant families to settle at the foot of Toompea hill, thereby sewing the seeds of a commercial capital. For the next 700 years, the descendants of these 'Baltic Germans' remained the dominant class both in the country and in the city.

A City Built on Salt

Tallinn's true heyday came in the 13th–16th centuries when it flourished as a major trading port on the route between East and West. This development into a booming merchant centre was kicked off in 1248, when the Danish king allowed Tallinn to adopt Lübeck Law, effectively making it a self-ruling city-state. What's more, around 1284 the city became a member of the Hanseatic League, a powerful association of cities that held a monopoly over northern European trade.

As the key Hansa port dealing with trade to Russia, Tallinn was a guaranteed success. Russian fur and wax, and Estonian grain and linen, were exported to cities in Western Europe, while textiles, herring, wine and spices went in the opposite direction. The most valuable commodity that came through Tallinn, however, was salt, said to be worth its weight in gold at the time. In fact, so much profitable salt cargo changed hands here on its way east that Tallinn became known as a city 'built on salt'.

It was during the boom years of the 1300s and 1400s that most of the present-day Old Town took shape. The city wall and towers were built and improved, workshops and warehouses sprung up, and a new Town Hall was installed in 1404 to house the City Council, the all-powerful body that controlled town life and international trade.

In 1346, Toompea's tenants changed. After the Estonians led a massive, but unsuccessful revolt called the St George's Night Uprising (1343–5), Denmark, which was then having its own internal difficulties, sold northern Estonia to the Riga-based German knights. Thus all of Estonia came under the control of the Livonian Order, which already ruled southern Estonia and present-day Latvia. In independent Tallinn however, the political changeover had little impact.

From Empire to Empire

Fortunes changed drastically in the mid-16th century with the outbreak of the Livonian War (1558–83). By now the Livonian state was in decline and, smelling blood, Russia, Sweden, Poland and Denmark all moved in for a share of the Baltic stakes. Tallinn and the nobles on Toompea negotiated surrender with Sweden in 1561, but the costly war would continue for two more decades.

The capital as it looked in 1615

The ensuing 'Swedish Period' of the nation's history is characterised by enlightened social policies, including more rights for peasants and the establishment of the nation's education system. But in the city itself, the situation had greatly deteriorated. Post-war plagues and famines caused Tallinn's population to plummet, and the city's role as a trade gateway to Russia had been taken over by competitors. The boom times were clearly over.

Conflict broke out again in the early 18th century, this time with imperial Sweden and an expansionist Russia fighting over Baltic territories in the devastating Great Northern War (1700–21). In 1710 Tsar Peter the Great captured Tallinn from the Swedes, and Estonia became a province of the Russian empire. Estonian peasants lost the privileges they had gained under Swedish rule and were forced into the same near slave-like serfdom practised in the rest of tsarist Russia.

National Awakening

'We shall never be great in number or strength, therefore we must become great in spirit' – pastor and linguist Jakob Hurt, a key figure in Estonia's National Awakening.

The 19th century, by contrast, brought huge improvements for ethnic Estonians. Serfdom was abolished in 1816, and from 1860 to 1880 a cultural revival referred to as the 'National Awakening' reached its height. Societies of 'Estophiles' promoted Estonian literature and culture, previously considered of little value. Estonian poetry bloomed, Estonian-language newspapers appeared, and the famous national epic, *Kalevipoeg*, was compiled. Now the nation that had for centuries been simply 'country people' started proudly calling themselves 'Estonians'.

At the same time, key political and demographic changes were happening. Completion of the St Petersburg–Tallinn railway line in 1870 brought a wave of industrial growth to Tallinn, and with it, thousands of ethnic Estonian and Russian factory workers. Germans were now outnumbered in the city, and in 1904, they lost municipal elections to an Estonian-Russian bloc. For the first time, non-Germans controlled Tallinn.

The Estonian Republic

On 24 February 1918, with the imperial Russian government ousted and World War I raging, Estonia declared independence. Before the new Estonian Republic became a reality, however, it would have to undergo half a year of German occupation, then fight a 13-month War of Independence against the Bolsheviks. But by 1920, the Estonians finally had their own state.

Life in the fledgling republic was far from perfect. The economic situation remained poor through the 1920s and early 30s, and strong political divisions between right and

The bastion known as Fat Margaret on fire, 1917

left extremists grew ever worse. In 1934, the head of state (and later president) Konstantin Päts and his supporters led a military coup d'état to keep ultra-nationalists from taking power. Though Päts stifled democracy and brought the country to near authoritarian rule, he remained a popular figure.

In the late 1930s, a long-awaited economic turn-around fuelled a building boom in Tallinn, and the republic's future looked bright.

World War and Occupation

World War II brought an end to the new country's aspirations. The Soviets occupied Estonia in June 1940, and immediately absorbed it into the USSR. A brutal year of arrests, executions and mass deportations to Siberian prison camps followed. Not surprisingly, when the Nazis drove out the Soviets at the end of 1941, the Estonians at first saw them as liberators. But their euphoria quickly died after it became clear that the

Germans wouldn't restore independence, and when the Nazi's own harsh policies came to light. During the three-year Nazi occupation, many Estonians were co-opted into the German Army, while others joined voluntarily, seeing it as their best chance to stave off another Soviet invasion.

The Soviet invasion came in September 1944, and thousands of Estonians fled in boats to Sweden, establishing a strong émigré community that kept the culture alive in exile. Around 30,000–35,000 others, known as the 'Forest Brothers', hid deep in Estonia's woods and started a 10-year campaign of resistance. The worst fears about renewed Soviet atrocities came to pass. After the war, 36,000 people were arrested and accused of aiding the Nazis, and over the next years, countless families were loaded onto cattle cars and sent to Siberia.

The Many Names of Tallinn

Tallinn has had many names. Its oldest recorded name is Qaleveni, as Arab cartographer al-Idrisi marked on his world map in 1154. Old Russian chronicles used the somewhat similar Kolyvan, which may come from the word *kaleva*, meaning 'solid' or 'strong', while Scandinavians probably referred to the city as Lindanise or Lindanaš. From the middle ages to the early 20th century it was known by the low-German name Reval (or, Rewel or Raevel), as the city was at the centre of the ancient Rävala county.

The name Tallinn originates from the period of Danish rule (1219–1346) when the city was referred to as *Castrum Danorum* (Danish Castle), which in Estonian was *tannin lidna*. A more widely held theory is that the name comes from a fusion of *Taani* (Danish) and *linn* (city), which first became Taanilinna and later Tallinn. After independence in 1918, the capital's official name was changed from Reval to Tallinn, but in 1925, the variation Tallinna was adopted. Finally, in 1933, it was changed back to Tallinn.

Conditions normalised somewhat in the 1950s, after the death of Joseph Stalin in 1953. Industries grew, and hundreds of thousands of ethnic Russians were relocated to Estonia, both to work in factories, and to 'Russify' the Soviet territory. Over the next decades, life was generally as stifled as it was in the rest of the USSR, but in many ways, the situation in Estonia was better than elsewhere. Supplies in shops were more regular, and Finnish TV broadcasts that could reach northern Estonia provided a window to the West.

Stalin toppled after the 'Singing Revolution'

The Singing Revolution

The seeds of Estonia's independence movement were sewn during the *perestroika* years of 1987 and 1988, when environmental protests quickly grew into mass demonstrations against the Soviet regime. Mass singing events held in June 1988, modelled on the National Song Festival, became the centre of a new national awakening, when more than 100,000 people packed Tallinn's festival grounds for several successive nights, singing traditional Estonian songs and calling for an end to the occupation. The events of the summer would be known as the 'Singing Revolution'. Estonia's Communist officialdom was on the demonstrators' side, increasingly calling for autonomy from Moscow. In a national referendum in March 1991, 78 percent of voters chose independence from the USSR.

On 20 August 1991, during a failed coup attempt in Moscow, the Supreme Soviet of the Republic of Estonia declared the nation's independence. Statues of Lenin immediately came down, and countries of the world, including the USSR, recognised Estonia's statehood. The Republic of Estonia was restored.

The 'Baltic tiger'

In the days following independence, Estonia faced the same dilemmas as the rest of the former USSR – organisational chaos, hyper-inflation, thousands of Russian troops on its soil and an environmental clean-up bill that would run into billions of dollars. But those bleak days did not last. Tough economic policies, combined with foreign investment, not only pulled Estonia out of the post-Soviet slump, but made this so-called 'Baltic tiger' a model of success for other newly independent countries in Europe.

Estonian girls dressed in traditional Muhu costume

Since 2004, Estonia has been a member of both the European Union and NATO. With all the economic and political roadblocks of the past finally removed, the nation is looking forward to a bright 21st century as a small but progressive Western democracy.

Historical Landmarks

1154 Tallinn first mentioned in historic records when Arab cartographer al-Idrisi marks it as a stronghold on his world map.

1219 King Valdemar II of Denmark conquers Estonian fortress on Toompea and uses it as a base to rule northern Estonia.

1227–38 Riga-based German crusaders wrest control of Tallinn and northern Estonia from the Danes; German merchants settle in Tallinn.

1248 Tallinn adopts Lübeck Law, to become a self-governing trade city.

1284 Tallinn becomes a member of the Hanseatic League.

1343–5 Estonian peasants stage bloody St George's Night Uprising, a massive, but ultimately unsuccessful rebellion against foreign rule.

1346 Danes sell their Estonian holdings to the German knights in Riga, putting Estonia under the rule of the Riga-based Livonian Order.

1558–83 Livonian War between Russia, Poland, Sweden and Denmark leaves Estonia under Swedish rule.

1684 Massive fire devastates Toompea.

1710 During the Great Northern War (1700–21), Sweden loses Estonia to the Russian Empire.

1816 Serfdom is abolished in Estonia.

1860–80 National Awakening.

1870 St Petersburg–Tallinn rail connection is completed, sparking rapid industrial growth.

1918 Estonia declares independence, which becomes de facto after a 13-month war against the Bolsheviks.

1940 Soviets invade, forcibly annexing Estonia into the USSR.

1941–3 Nazi invasion and occupation.

1944 Soviet forces reinvade; a half-century of Soviet occupation follows.

1980 Tallinn hosts the yachting events of the Moscow Olympic Games.

1987–8 Mass protests against Soviet rule, later to be collectively called the 'Singing Revolution'.

1991 Estonia regains independence.

1994 Last Russian troops leave Estonian soil.

2004 Estonia joins NATO and the European Union.

WHERE TO GO

W hen arriving in Tallinn, most visitors' first instinct is to head straight into the Old Town – and rightly so. This tightly packed ensemble of winding, cobblestone streets, beautiful medieval dwellings, breathtaking church spires, café-filled squares and mysterious, half-hidden courtyards isn't just Tallinn's biggest tourist draw, it's also the heart and soul of the city. Better still, it's all neatly pack-aged within a centuries-old town wall, giving it a fairytale-like charm and at the same time making it relatively easy to navigate and explore.

Today the Old Town looks like one big, medieval mosaic, but it's actually made up of what were historically two dis-tinct entities – Toompea Hill, home of the gentry and the representatives of Estonia's ruling power, and the Lower Town, an autonomous Hanseatic trading city populated by merchants and craftsmen. This guide thoroughly covers both of these areas and directs readers to the most intriguing parts of the city centre, the nearby neighbourhood of Kadri-org, and the outlying districts.

Our tour appropriately starts at the very top, on Toompea, the birthplace of Tallinn.

TOOMPEA

Take one look down from the edge of this 24-m (78-ft) lime-stone hill and you'll understand why Toompea (Dome Hill) has always been synonymous with power. Not only did its steep slopes provide a natural defence against would-be invaders, the high elevation gave it a commanding view of the comings and goings in the harbour nearby. It's no wonder

View of St Olav's Church from Toompea Hill

then that ancient Estonians picked this spot to build a wooden stronghold, now thought to be Tallinn's earliest settlement. That fortress is long gone, but the tradition it started has continued. From the Danes in 1219 to the Russians in the early 20th century, every foreign empire that ruled the northern Estonian lands has used Toompea as its power base, stationing its political representatives in Toompea Castle.

The fortified area outside the castle, meanwhile, was home to Estonia's gentry. German landlords, owners of feudal estates in the surrounding countryside, built grand, often palatial houses on Toompea from where they would look down, both literally and figuratively, on the busy merchants and workers in the Lower Town. Today most of these houses are embassies, government offices or extremely high-priced flats.

Given Toompea's history as the seat of the ruling power, it's somehow fitting that both Estonia's Parliament and its

Toompea Castle with the Pikk Hermann (Tall Hermann) Tower

government administration are now located here. What draws tourists to Toompea isn't these grand institutions though, it's the prospect of seeing two of the nation's most spectacular churches and getting the best views of Tallinn.

> **Pikk Jalg is so steep that anyone driving a carriage downward was in for a harrowing experience. Before the carriage started off, coachmen and tower guards had to shout to each other to ensure that the area at the bottom was clear of traffic.**

Pikk Jalg and Lühike Jalg

Four roads and four stairways lead up to Toompea, but by far the most interesting paths up the hill are Tallinn's two 'legs' – **Pikk jalg** ('Long Leg' Street) and **Lühike jalg** ('Short Leg' Street).

In medieval times, if you were travelling by horse or carriage, you would have taken Pikk jalg to reach Toompea from the Lower Town. It starts at the end of Pikk Street at the curious-looking **Long Leg Gate Tower** (Pika jala väravatorn) and continues in a straight, steady climb upward to **Castle Square** (Lossi plats). The four-sided gate tower was built in 1380, but its present shape comes from a mid-15th-century reconstruction. Pikk jalg itself is a favourite haunt of local artists vying to sell their works to passing tourists. High above the artists' heads, the extravagant mansions along the edge of the cliff serve as a good indication of the wealth and power of Toompea's gentry.

Along the opposite side of Pikk jalg you will see a high defensive wall built in 1454–5 and known as the **Wall of Hatred**. Tensions between the Lower Town and Toompea often ran high in medieval times, with the merchants and artisans in the Hanseatic city fearing raids from their neighbours on the hill. This animosity accounts for the need for the wall and the gate towers on Pikk jalg and Lühike jalg, and for the fact that the gates separating Toompea and Lower Town were kept closed and locked at night.

Picturesque Lühike jalg was historically the main pedestrian passage into Toompea. Though officially a street, this is really just a narrow, winding lane with a staircase. Today it is flanked on both sides by some of Tallinn's more intriguing art shops, and is also home to the **Adamson-Eric Museum** (open Wed–Sun 11am–6pm; admission charge), which showcases works of Adamson Eric (1902–68) one of the most outstanding Estonian painters and applied artists of the 20th century.

At the top of the street's 16-m (52-ft) climb stands the **Short Leg Gate Tower** (Lühikese jala väravatorn), built in

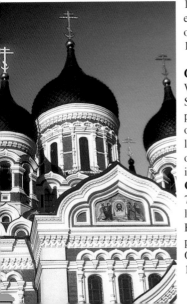

Aleksander Nevski Cathedral

1456. The tower was extensively renovated in the late 1980s, but the sturdy, wooden door you pass here is original and dates from the 17th century.

Orthodox Cathedral

When you reach Castle Square at the top of Toompea, you come to a dramatic, onion-domed church that looks like something straight out of a Russian novel. This is the **Aleksander Nevski Cathedral** (open daily 8am–7pm), the most impressive-looking Orthodox church in Estonia and an important place of worship for Tallinn's Orthodox faithful. Built from 1894 to 1900, the cathedral is a relatively new addition to Toompea. It was designed by St Petersburg architect Mikhail Preobrazhensky and follows the same basic layout as the five-domed churches that started to appear in Moscow and Jaroslavl in the 17th century.

Cathedral interior

Though the cathedral serves a purely spiritual purpose these days, it was originally placed here as a blatant symbol of Russian power. In the late 19th century, imperial Russia was carrying out an intense campaign of Russification in its outer provinces. As part of its drive to assert cultural dominance over the mainly Lutheran Germans and Estonians, the tsarist government built this towering Orthodox cathedral directly in front of the castle, right on what had been one of the city's most famous squares. In doing so, builders also had to remove a statue of Martin Luther that stood here.

As a further symbolic blow, the cathedral was dedicated to Prince Aleksander Nevski, the Russian hero whose forces famously defeated the Baltic-based German crusaders in the 'Battle on Ice' on Lake Peipsi in 1242. Nevski is depicted in the elaborate **mosaic** on the south side of the cathedral, while the mosaic on the north side shows Count Vsevlod of Pskov, who led successful raids against the Estonians in the 13th century.

A chance to look at the cathedral's interior shouldn't be passed up. Visitors are welcome to come in and view the abundance of awe-inspiring **icons**, mosaics and other works of religious art that line the walls. The cathedral also operates a small gift shop to the right of the entrance.

Toompea Castle

Next to the cathedral stands a large pink edifice that bears a distinctly regal look. This is the front of **Toompea Castle** (Toompea Loss), historic seat of power in Estonia and home to the *Riigikogu*, Estonia's parliament. The castle's origins go back to 1227–9 when the Knights of the Sword built a square fortress here which they surrounded with a circular, stone wall. In the 14th century this was rebuilt into a convent-style fortress with a trapezoidal inner courtyard, 20-m (65-ft) high walls, and four corner towers, three of which are still standing. The **baroque palace** you see in front of you was built from 1767 to 73 on the order of Russian Empress Catherine the Great, and served as the administration building for the Russ-

---

Kalev's Grave

According to legend, Toompea is actually the burial mound of Kalev, the mythical figure who founded Tallinn. When Kalev died, his grief-stricken widow Linda started to cover his grave with stone after stone, and the poor woman kept at it until she had created this bulging hill.

During the construction of the Aleksander Nevski Cathedral, a rumour surfaced that workers digging the space for the foundations had stumbled onto Kalev's grave. They supposedly uncovered an iron door bearing the inscription 'Cursed be anyone who dares disturb my peace' – not very original as curses go, but nevertheless enough to worry the locals. As building continued, cracks started to appear in the cathedral's foundations. People took this as a sign of impending doom either for the cathedral or for Tallinn as a whole. Luckily, the much-feared disaster never came to pass.

Toompea Castle walls and the Dome Church

ian provincial government in Estonia during tsarist times. The three-storey **Parliament Building** in the courtyard, not visible from the outside, was built in 1920–2 on the foundations of the former convent and reflects an Expressionist style.

Tourists aren't allowed in the castle itself, but anyone can visit the peaceful **Governor's Garden** to the left of the castle. This is the best place to view another Tallinn landmark, **Tall Hermann** (Pikk Hermann) tower. The tower was built onto the corner of the castle in 1371, but only reached its final 46-m (150-ft) height after reconstruction in 1500. Tradition dictates that whichever nation flies its flag on Tall Hermann rules Estonia. On 24 February 1989, in what was one of the boldest gestures of Estonia's push for independence from the USSR, the Estonian blue, black and white flag was raised here in place of the red Soviet one. Estonia's colours have flown on Tall Hermann every day since – a potent symbol of the nation's sovereignty.

To see the castle's most medieval-looking side, you can take a quick detour down Falgi Street, south of the fortress, and then return to Toompea to see more of the town's old defences.

Kiek in de Kök

Take the steps leading down from the south side of Aleksander Nevski Cathedral and continue through a small park. Here you'll see a large, round medieval tower that looks like it could stand up to any amount of cannon fire. This is **Kiek in de Kök**, the Baltic region's most powerful cannon tower. Its name, which in Low German literally means 'peek into the kitchen',

Kiek in de Kök

refers to the tower's 36-m (118-ft) height. Soldiers posted here joked that they could see right down the chimneys and into the kitchens of the houses below.

Kiek in de Kök was built in 1475–6 as a much smaller tower, and then almost immediately rebuilt to give it its current mammoth size. It was finally put to the test during the Livonian War (1558–83) when Ivan the Terrible's forces besieged Tallinn twice. Though the tower stood up fairly well and played a decisive role in keeping the attackers out of the city, Russian cannons managed to blow a massive hole in its top floor. According to historic accounts, the hole was so large that two oxen could have fitted through it side by side. During post-war repairs, builders set six **stone cannon balls** in the tower's outer wall as a memorial. These can still be seen on its southeast side.

Now the tower operates as a **museum** (open Mar–Oct Tues–Sun 10.30am–5.30pm; Nov–Feb Tues–Sun 11am–5pm; admission charge) displaying the development of

Danish King's Garden

the town and its defences from the 13th to the 18th century. Apart from seeing the displays, which are somewhat haphazard and dated, a visit here will allow you to climb the old staircases that run through the tower's 4-m (13-ft) thick walls and enjoy the dizzying view from the top floor.

Danish King's Garden

On the way back to Castle Square you can get a good look at more towers by following the thick town wall on the right. Crossing through a rectangular passage in the wall you come to the **Danish King's Garden** (Taani kuninga aed). According to legend, this is the birthplace of the Danish flag. King Valdemar II supposedly camped on this spot when his forces were first trying to conquer Toompea in 1219. The Danes were losing the battle when suddenly the skies opened up and a red flag with a white cross floated downward from the heavens. Spurred on by this miraculous sign, the Danes were able to fight on to victory.

The two towers here, the small, round **Stable Tower** (Tallitorn) and the larger, square **Maiden's Tower** (Neitsitorn), both date from the 14th century. The name 'Maiden's Tower' is an exercise in medieval irony – the tower was actually a prison for prostitutes.

Dome Church

Both Toom-Kooli Street and Piiskopi Street lead from Castle Square to **Church Square** (Kiriku plats), home to the majestic-looking **Dome Church** (Toomkirik), which is the headquarters of the Lutheran church of Estonia. Officially called the **Cathedral of St Mary the Virgin**, the Dome Church was probably established not long after the Danes arrived in Toompea in 1219. Records first mention the church in 1233, by which time Dominican monks had already replaced the original wooden structure with one constructed of stone. The church's vaulted main body is thought to originate from a 14th-century rebuilding.

The Dome Church

In 1684 a devastating fire ripped through Toompea destroying nearly every building, including the Dome Church. Though the church was operating again two years later, reconstruction work took until the end of the century. The **baroque**

tower was a later addition; it dates from 1778–9.

Once you step into the church you'll probably be standing on a large **burial slab** inscribed with the name Otto Johann Thuve, also known as 'Tallinn's Don Juan'. According to legend, Thuve was an inveterate playboy who loved parties, wine and, in particu-

> After Toompea burned in 1684, there was so much rubble in the area that the ground level was raised by more than a metre. Because workers used the original floor when rebuilding Dome Church, anyone now entering the church has to take several steps down from street level.

lar, women. Just before he died in 1696, he requested that he be buried in this spot. His hope was that people would step on him when entering the church, and by doing so help wash away his sins.

The most striking aspect of the church's interior is the huge collection of funereal **coats of arms** covering the walls. These intricate works of art, dating mostly from the 17th to the 20th century, traditionally accompanied the casket during funeral processions, and were later kept in the church as a memorial. Most reflect a baroque style, as does the rest of the church's interior. The intricate **baroque pulpit** and **high altar** were both carved by the Tallinn sculptor Christian Ackermann and completed in 1696.

Along the northern wall, opposite the entrance, are the lavish **tombs** of some fairly eminent historic figures. These include Pontus de la Gardie (died 1585), French-born head of Swedish forces during the Livonian War; A.J. von Krusenstern (died 1848), a Baltic German explorer who was the first to circumnavigate the globe under the Russian flag; and Admiral Samuel Greig of Fife, Scotland (1735–88), commander of Russia's Baltic Fleet and reputed lover of Catherine the Great.

Just outside the church is a green, two-storey, Renaissance-style building called the **Knighthood House** (Rüütelkonna hoone). It was built in 1848 to serve as a meeting place for the Knighthood, an organisation that acted as a kind of class authority of Toompea's gentry. The building was home to Estonia's foreign ministry during the first independence, and the Estonian National Library during Soviet times. Until 2005 the Knighthood House served as the main building of the Estonian Art Museum, which moved its collection to a purpose-built complex in Kadriorg Park *(see page 60)*.

The towers of Tallinn from Patkuli viewing platform

Viewing Platforms

Heading to the right of the Knighthood House and down Kohtu Street will take you past some impressive neoclassical and neohistorical houses once owned by Toompea's noble elite. The street soon ends at the **Kohtu Street viewing platform**. From here there is a truly spectacular view of the red-tiled roofs of the medieval Lower Town as well as the modern-looking city beyond the town walls.

The roof in the immediate foreground with the cockerel-shaped weather vane belongs to the Long Leg Gate Tower, its fairytale look contrasting sharply with the blocky, white Viru Hotel behind it. The tall, medieval church on the left towards the port is St Olav's Church; the one much closer and on the right is St Nicholas's Church. Among the buildings in the centre of the Lower Town, you can make out the two very similar towers of the Town Hall and the Holy Spirit Church.

Further in the distance, beyond the high-rise hotels and office blocks, you can make out the arched rim of the **Tallinn Song Festival Arena** and the triangle-shaped ruins of **St Bridget's Convent**. The spire on the horizon is Tallinn's **TV Tower**, and the rows of giant apartment blocks to its right mark the suburb of Lasnamäe.

The Town Wall

Stone barricades had been established around Tallinn as early as 1265, but the town wall's current shape comes from an extensive reconstruction undertaken in the 14th century. The wall was continually improved through the years and, by its heyday in the 16th century, it was 2.4km (1½ miles) long, 14–16m (46–52 feet) high, up to about 3m (10ft) thick, and had a total of 46 towers. Today 1.9km (1¼ miles) of the wall are still standing, as are 20 defence towers, two inner gate towers, and sections of two outer gate towers.

The closest segment of the wall you see from the Patkuli viewing platform, connecting **Nunna**, **Sauna** and **Kuldjala** towers, is open to tourists. A visit here is the best way to see Tallinn's defences up close and to enjoy wonderful views of Toompea. When in the Lower Town, follow your map to the corner of Gümnaasiumi and Suur-Kloostri, and look for the entrance to the **Town Wall** (Linnamüür; open June–Aug Mon–Fri 11am–7pm, Sat–Sun 11am–4pm; April–May, Sept Tues–Fri noon–6pm, Sat–Sun 11am–4pm; Oct–Nov, Jan–Mar Wed–Fri noon–5pm, Sat–Sun 11am–4pm; Dec–Feb Fri–Sun 11am–4pm; admission charge).

A slightly different view is on offer at the nearby **Patkuli viewing platform**, which can be reached by turning right on Toom-Rüütli, then left at the end of that street onto a nearly hidden passage. This platform looks over the northern section of the Lower Town and affords an excellent view, taking in St Olav's Church, the **town wall** and several of its **towers**.

The lavish manor house standing on the cliff immediately to the left of the platform is **Stenbock House** (Stenbocki maja). Built in the late 18th century, it has been a courthouse and, at one time, a private home. After years of Soviet-era dilapidation it was restored in the 1990s and is now the office of the Government of Estonia.

From the Patkuli viewing platform you can head straight down Rahukohtu Street to continue touring Toompea, or make your way down the **Patkuli Steps** and into the Lower Town.

LOWER TOWN

For most visitors, it is Lower Town (All-Linn) that defines Tallinn. This is where the crowds mingle, where shops, cafés and restaurants light up the medieval streets, where tourists come to gaze at historic curiosities of every sort or to simply relax and take in the timeless atmosphere of the Old Town. In short, this is where life happens in Tallinn.

Town Hall Square, the hub of activity in Tallinn

In that respect, little has changed since medieval times. The area we now call the Lower Town was then the Hanseatic city of Tallinn (or Reval as it was known at the time), a busy trading city of international stature. In 1248 it was granted autonomous status and from then on had its own government, local laws, social institutions and defence forces. More importantly, it was the domain of merchants and artisans, labourers and servants, all of whom would have contributed to the general bustle of commerce as they went about their daily routines.

Centuries of activity have left the Lower Town with a wealth of fascinating sights, many of which are nicely com-plemented by the museums, cafés and other businesses oper-

ating among them. A popular – and perfectly reasonable – way to make your way through this maze of curiosities is to put away your map and let your feet lead you where they may. That said, your wandering will be all the richer if you arm yourself with inside information on these attractions.

Town Hall Square

For at least seven centuries, the social and cultural heart of Tallinn has been **Town Hall Square** (Raekoja plats), the attractive open area at the centre of the Old Town. In medieval times it served as the town's main marketplace and was also

---

Crime and Punishment

In addition to the other functions it had in medieval times, Town Hall Square served as a place of public punishment. For example, women accused of gossiping were sentenced to walk around the square three times while enduring the whistling and jeering of the crowds. Look for the iron shackles that are mounted on one pillar of the Town Hall. These were used to punish people guilty of petty crimes such as swindling and non-payment of debts. In more serious cases, convicts would be locked in a pillory that once stood on the square.

The town also employed an executioner, but as a rule the executions took place on a hill outside the town. One notable exception occurred in the late 17th century. A drunken priest named Panicke ordered an omelette at an inn, and finding it 'hard as the sole of a shoe', sent it back. Upon being served two more such horrendous omelettes, he grabbed an axe and slaughtered the waitress. Once sober, the priest turned himself in, begging to be executed. So heinous was his crime that the sentence was carried out immediately, right on the square. Two long stones in the shape of an 'L', not far from the Town Hall Pharmacy, mark the place where he was beheaded, though the spot may be covered by café tables in summer.

the site of tournaments, festivals and even an execution. Even now the square acts as the chief gathering place for the city's residents, each year hosting scores of concerts, art markets and festival events. Town Hall Square is invariably packed with umbrella-shaded café terraces in spring and summer, and every winter it's home to Tallinn's Christmas Tree, a tradition that dates back to 1441.

The Town Hall by night

Presiding over the square is Tallinn's **Town Hall** (Raekoda; open July–Aug Mon–Sat 10am–4pm; admission charge). Historic records indicate that another town hall occupied this spot as early as 1322, but the late-Gothic structure you see today was completed in 1404. **Old Thomas** (Vana Toomas), the soldier-shaped weather vane perched atop the spire, has been watching over the city since 1530, while the baroque spire itself and the fanciful, dragon-shaped drainpipes both date from 1627.

Tallinn's powerful Town Council would hold meetings on the hall's main floor upstairs, where the beautiful, vaulted **Citizens' Hall** and **Council Chamber** are located. The wooden benches that occupy them are decorated with intricate, medieval carvings that easily qualify as art treasures. The ground floor, by contrast, was more a place of business, encompassing a trading hall, treasury and counting room, while the building's basement housed a torture chamber. Unforunately, the Town Hall is open to drop-in visitors only during July and August, but group visits can be arranged for all

The Town Hall Pharmacy (left)

other times of the year (tel: 6457 900). Anyone not afraid of heights should also climb the 64-m (210-ft) **Town Hall Tower** (Raekoja torn; open 15 May–30 Aug daily 11am–6pm; admission fee) for a great view of the Old Town.

Tucked behind the Town Hall is the 15th-century **Town Hall Prison** (Rae-vangla) where those arrested were kept before trial. It now houses an interesting **Museum of Photography** (open Mar–Oct Mon–Tues, Thur–Sun 10am–6pm; Nov–Feb Mon, Thu–Sun 10am–5pm; admission charge) chronicling 150 years of Tallinn's photographic pursuits and displaying numerous antique cameras. A few of the exhibits occupy the old cells, downstairs.

Back on Town Hall Square you'll see thousands of stones covering the ground, but there is one of particular interest – a large, round slab decorated with a compass rose. You can find it by standing at the corner of the Town Hall, directly in front of the café. Look for a seam in the pattern of bricks and follow it 25 or 30 paces out into the square until you reach the unmistakeable spot. Tour guides call this stone the **Centre of Tallinn**, a name that isn't based so much on geography as it is on the fact that you can theoretically see the tops of all five of the Old Town's spires from here. Be prepared to stretch, bend and/or jump to achieve this goal.

In a corner of the square opposite the Town Hall stands the **Town Hall Pharmacy** (Raeapteek), one of the oldest, continuously running pharmacies in Europe. Records first mention it in 1422, but it may have been established decades earlier. Amazingly, from 1580 to 1911 the pharmacy was managed by 10 generations of the same family. Some of the useful preparations sold here in centuries past include minced bat, burnt bees, snakeskin and powdered unicorn horn. Everyday items such as paper, wax, gunpowder and claret were available as well.

These days you'll find the same remedies here as in any modern pharmacy, but in homage to its history, the location maintains a small **exhibition room** (open Mon–Fri 9am–7pm, Sat 9am–5pm; free) displaying antique pharmacy equipment, archaic medicines and similar artefacts.

Holy Spirit Church

Just a few paces north of Town Hall Square through Saiakang passage stands a radiant, white church with an octagonal tower. This is the **Holy Spirit Church** (Püha Vaimu kirik; open May–Sept Mon–Sat 10am–4pm, Oct–Apr Mon–Fri 10am–3pm; admission charge), tiny in comparison to the Old Town's other medieval churches, but enormous in the hearts of ordinary Estonians for the role it played in their cultural history. It was here that the very first sermons were given in the Estonian language after the Reformation, and in 1535 the church's pastor, Johann Koell, translated and published what's thought to be the first book in Estonian.

The church was important to Tallinn's medieval administration: it served as a chapel for the Town Council, and one of its rooms was used for signing contracts and treaties, the sanctity of the church ensuring the subsequent honesty of all parties. Mostly, however, this was a church for the common folk. As early as the 13th century it operated an almshouse tending to the city's sick, elderly and poor, and in contrast to other churches, the Holy Spirit Church's congregation was made up of Tallinn's lower class.

The building was completed in the 1360s and its overall shape dates from that period. Its **baroque spire**, however, is a newer installation; it was added after a major fire in 1684 destroyed its Renaissance-style predecessor. This spire recently underwent extensive renovation – another fire in 2002, which fortunately was confined to the tower, partially melted the spire's base, and much of its copper had to be replaced. The most eye-catching addition to the church is the large, blue-and-gold **clock** on the exterior of the building near the main doorway. Created by Tallinn's best-known woodcarver, Christian Ackermann, in the late 17th-century, this is the city's oldest – and by far most captivating – public timepiece. The figures you see in each of its corners represent the four apostles.

Keeping time at the Holy Spirit Church

As attractive as both the spire and clock are, the church's most impressive feature is unquestionably its rich interior. Decorated from almost floor to ceiling with lavishly carved woodwork, including baroque pews and a Renaissance pulpit, the ensemble is truly awe-inspiring. One could spend hours examining painted panels on its side galleries. The church's best-loved piece is the **altar**, commissioned from the renowned Lübeck sculptor and painter, Bernt Notke, in 1483. Figures of the Virgin Mary with child, apostles and saints, all painted in bright, clear blue, red and gold, stand at the centre of the cupboard-type altarpiece.

The Guilds

Leading from the area just north of Town Hall Square to the northernmost tip of the Old Town is the aptly named Pikk Street, or 'Long Street'. It was the longest street in medieval Tallinn, a busy artery connecting the port to the town's main marketplace. Not only was it the principal route for merchants visiting Tallinn, it also was home to several guild associations.

From the 14th century, guilds, all-important associations of merchants and craftsmen, played a major role in town politics and society. Though many guilds took on the character of religious brotherhoods, they were actually profession-based organisations that acted as both trade unions and social clubs. They regulated who could or could not practise a particular trade, and they protected their members' interests, often by pressuring the Town Council to enact regulations in their favour. Equally important, the guilds were the architects of Tallinn's social life, organising weddings, feasts and public celebrations. Membership in a guild also determined social status, and only members of the better guilds were allowed to wear more opulent clothes.

The grand looking building at Pikk 17, just across from the Holy Spirit Church is the **Great Guild Hall** (Suurgildi hoone), which served as a meeting place for Tallinn's Great Guild, a wealthy association of merchants that wielded considerable influence over town affairs. The hall was completed around 1410 and has changed little since that time. The red and white symbols on its façade represent the guild's coat of arms, and the fanciful, lion's-head doorknockers date from 1430. The hall is now home to a branch of the **Estonian History Museum** (open Thur–Tues 11am–6pm; admission charge), which chronicles the nation's developments from prehistoric times up to the 18th century.

Further along and on the right-hand side of the street you'll see the eccentric façade of the **Dragon Gallery**, with its sea-horse-tailed serpents and Egyptian slaves. Created by Tartu-born Jacques Rosenbaum in 1910, this is by far the most memorable art nouveau façade in Tallinn.

The Cat's Well

Tallinn wasn't always the most animal-friendly place in times past. On the corner of Rataskaevu and Dunkri streets stands a picturesque, covered wheel well, the subject of countless tourist snapshots. Few visitors who pass by here realise that the well has a highly unsavoury legend attached to it.

In medieval times, local residents believed that a water spirit lived in the well, and that it would become angry and flood the town if they didn't give it regular animal sacrifices. So all sorts of animals – mostly dead but some living – were thrown down the well. The main victims of this superstitious practice were stray neighbourhood cats, giving rise to the well's popular nickname, 'Cat's Well'.

The practice did little to improve the quality of the water drawn from here, though in reality, the problem may have had more to do with a high lime content. In either case, the well fell into disuse by the 19th century and was filled in.

The bright, triple-gabled **Kanut Guild Hall** (Kanuti gildi hoone) stands next door to it at Pikk 20. This was home to the Kanut Guild, which united skilled craftsmen from a number of different trades. The house's present, Tudor-style appearance comes from an 1860s remodelling, its overall look inspired by English Gothic architecture. The two bold-looking statues on its façade represent St Kanut and Martin Luther. The house is now used as a dance theatre.

Brotherhood of Blackheads doorway

High up, across the street from the Kanut Guild Hall is the somewhat bizarre figure of a **monocle-wearing man** gazing down. There are several theories as to why he was put here; the most amusing is that a jealous wife installed it to break her husband's habit of spying on the ladies as they practised ballet in the upper floors of the guild hall.

At Pikk 26 you come to the eye-catching **House of the Brotherhood of Blackheads** (Mustpeade vennaskonna hoone; open daily 10am–7pm; free). The brotherhood, a guild of young, unmarried merchants, played a major role in medieval Tallinn's life and politics, organising the town's defence and, among other duties, arranging annual tournaments and celebrations. The guild's curious name comes from the fact that its patron saint, St Mauritius, was a dark-skinned Moor. The exquisite Renaissance façade dates from 1597, and its beautiful, carved wood door, one of the most recognised architectural elements in Tallinn, was installed in 1640. The house is now used as a concert hall, but when no events are scheduled, visitors can drop in to look at its gorgeous, vaulted White Hall and Olav's Hall, as well as an intriguing, indoor courtyard.

KGB Headquarters

A careful observer will notice something eerie about the building at Pikk 59. Its cellar windows are completely bricked over – a detail that gives it a decidedly ominous appearance. This was the **KGB Headquarters** during the Soviet period. In this sad place many people were tortured and shot; others were interrogated before being sent to Siberia. Now it's used as a police administration building. The placard on the front of the building reads, 'This building housed the headquarters of the organ of repression of the Soviet occupational power. Here began the road to suffering for thousands of Estonians.'

> **During Soviet times, the neighbouring KGB office used St Olav's metal spire *(below)* as an antenna for their radio communications.**

St Olav's Church

Just a few paces further on is Tallinn's largest medieval structure, the enormous **St Olav's Church** (Oleviste kirik). A short walk around its side, towards Lai Street,

The Three Sisters

will give you a better view of its sheer magnitude. The church was first mentioned in historic records in 1267, and originally served a Scandinavian merchants' camp that occupied this end of Pikk Street in the 13th century. The basic shape it has today, however, comes from rebuilding undertaken in the 15th century.

In 1500, an absurdly tall (159m/522ft), Gothic-style pavilion steeple was built on to the top of the tower, making St Olav's Church the tallest building in the world at the time. The hope was that the huge steeple would act as a helpful signpost for ships approaching the busy, commercial town. The steeple indeed proved to be a useful advertising tool, but it turned out to be even more effective as a lightning rod. Numerous bolts of lightning struck the steeple through the centuries, and twice, once in 1625 and again in 1820, the church was burned to the ground. The steeple you now see was installed after the first fire, and is only 124m (407ft) tall, a whole 25m (82ft) shorter than the original. In spring and summer, able-bodied visitors can make the arduous climb to the top of the **church tower** (open Apr–Oct daily 10am–6pm; admission charge) for spectacular views of Toompea and the Old Town.

The Great Coast Gate and Vicinity

Humbler in size than the church but just as awe-inspiring is **The Three Sisters** (Kolm õde), at Pikk 71, a magnificently restored ensemble made up of three brightly painted, 15th-

Fat Margaret's Tower

century terraced houses. Each of these is a bit smaller than the next, creating the impression of 'sisters'. The houses and their beautiful façades – including an intricate, baroque front door from 1651 – are striking examples of medieval architecture. The Three Sisters now operate as a luxury hotel.

The street ends at the **Great Coast Gate** (Suur Rannavärav). This and the Viru Gates on Viru Street are all that remain of the six powerful, medieval gates that once regulated access to Tallinn. The Great Coast Gate – actually a collection of towers and gates – was founded in the early 1300s, but its largest and most famous piece, **Fat Margaret's Tower** (Paks Margareeta), was built from 1511 to 1530. The squat, round cannon tower can best be seen from outside the gate. With a diameter of 25m (82ft) and walls that were up to 5m (17ft) thick, the tower was a formidable part of the town's defences.

The tower now houses the **Estonian Maritime Museum** (Eesti Meremuuseum; open Wed–Sun 10am–6pm; admission charge), with four floors presenting an extensive look at the nation's seafaring history from Neolithic times to the present. Visitors can climb to the roof for sweeping views of the town and harbour. On the grassy hill outside the tower you'll see a row of medieval cannons, and a large monument

in the shape of an incomplete bridge. The latter is a memorial to the victims of the *Estonia* ferry disaster. The 15,000-
tonne ferry sank en route from Tallinn to Stockholm on 28
September 1994, and 852 people died.

From here steps lead down to Uus Street and the curious
Mine Museum (Miinimuuseum; open Wed–Sun 9am–5pm;
admission charge). Estonia's coast has been a treasure-trove of
explosive marine mines from various countries, some dating
back as far as the late 1800s. More mines are constantly being
found and deactivated, and many are put on display here.

The Latin Quarter

The area at the end of Vene Street has come to be called
Tallinn's 'Latin Quarter' thanks to the presence of a Dominican
Monastery that operated here from the 13th to the 16th century.
The monastery itself, or what remains of it, is still the area's
prime attraction, but these days a number of newer sights add
to the fascinating milieu of this corner of the Old Town.

One example can be found at the far end of Vene Street
in the form of the impressive **St Nicholas's Orthodox
Church** (Püha Nikolai Imetegija kirik). This neoclassical,
Russian Orthodox church, with its copper dome and double
towers, was built in the 1820s by St Petersburg architect
Luigi Rusca. Visitors shouldn't be afraid to look inside
at the iconostasis, said to rival the most beautiful in Estonia. Across the street from the church, at Vene 17, a well-
restored medieval dwelling house is home to the **Tallinn
City Museum** (Tallinna Linnamuuseum; open March–Oct
Mon, Wed–Sun 10am–6pm; Nov–Feb Mon, Wed–Sun
10am–5pm; admission charge). This is by far the city's
most modern and complete history museum. Eye-catching
exhibits use life-sized re-creations, text, sound and video to
chronicle the city's development from its founding right up
to post-Soviet times.

➤ Vene Street's main draw is the **Dominican Monastery** (Dominiklaste hoor; courtyard at Vene 16 open 15 May– 30 Sept daily 9.30am– 6pm; museum at Müürivahe 33 open 15 May–30 Sept daily 10am–5pm; admission fee). Known as St Catherine's Monastery, it was founded here in 1246 by the Dominican Order and, until the Reformation, played a key role in the town's religious affairs. The monastery wasn't always popular with Tallinn's ruling elite, however, because the monks' work was often too supportive of the common Estonian people. The monastery was closed down after the Reformation in 1525, and in 1531 the abandoned complex was ravaged by fire.

Now all that remains of the monastery are the **courtyard** and a few of its surrounding hallways and chambers. A visit here is nevertheless a fascinating look at Tallinn's early history. Visitors to the monastery's beautiful courtyard can roam its ancient corridors and gain an impression of monastic life in medieval times. These same corridors now also display a fascinating collection of **medieval stonemasonry** salvaged from elsewhere in the Old Town. A separate museum, whose entrance is at Müürivahe 33, around the corner, gives access to the monastery's inner chambers. Exhibits here include additional stone carvings as well as archaeological finds from the monastery grounds. The mysterious '**energy pillar**' in its cellar is believed to give off a kind of psychic force.

➤ Tallinn's most picturesque lane, **St Catherine's Passage** (Katariina käik), connects Vene and Müürivahe streets just south of the monastery. A long row of 15th–17th-century structures on one side of the passage houses **St Catherine's Guild** (Katariina gild), where a group of women artists use traditional methods to create modern-looking and sometimes off-beat handicrafts. Visitors can drop in and watch them working away on quilts, ceramics, glass, silk designs, jewellery and fine leatherwork. The opposite side of the passage

St Catherine's Passage

displays some intriguing – if somewhat eerie – stone burial slabs that were removed from the former St Catherine's Church, directly behind them, during renovation.

St Nicholas's Church
St Nicholas's Church (Niguliste kirik), which looks proudly over Harju Street, was the only church in the Lower Town not to be ransacked during the Reformation of 1524, thanks to its head of congregation who successfully kept the mobs out by pouring molten lead into the locks. Dedicated to the patron saint of merchants and artisans, it was founded by a group of German settlers who had set up a trading yard here in the early 13th century. Because it was built before Tallinn's town wall was completed, the church was outfitted with heavy wooden beams to bar the doors and hiding places for those escaping attack. The main body and choir were modernised in the 15th century, but the appearance the church has now is

the result of constant rebuilding since then. The church was destroyed in the Soviet bombing raid of March 1944 *(see panel below)*, but it was painstakingly reconstructed from 1956 to 1984.

St Nicholas's now serves a purely secular function, operating as the **Niguliste Museum and Concert Hall** (open Wed–Sun 10am–5pm; admission charge), which showcases religious art from Estonia and abroad. Art lovers should definitely not pass up an opportunity to visit this fascinating church-turned-museum. It has the distinction of containing Estonia's most famous work of art, 15th-century artist Bernt Notke's mural *Dance Macabre* (Dance with Death), a frightening masterpiece depicting people from various walks of

Bombing Ruins

Most Old Town sights focus on Tallinn's medieval past, but a walk down Harju Street just a few metres from Town Hall Square reveals a very different aspect of the city's history. Here the relative blandness of surrounding buildings and the barren area stretching to neighbouring Rüütli Street are both testaments to the devastation of World War II.

On 9 March 1944, with Nazi Germany still occupying Estonia, the Soviet Air Force bombed Tallinn, killing more than 500 people, destroying entire neighbourhoods and leaving 20,000 homeless. The area of Old Town hardest hit was Harju Street, where an entire block was reduced to rubble. Beyond the fence on the west side of the street you can see the bombing ruins, remains of cellars where several buildings, including a hotel and a cinema, once stood. After the war, the Soviet Government covered this up – both literally and figuratively – by turfing over the scene and blaming the destruction on the Germans. In the summer of 1988, with the independence movement brewing, the area was excavated and signs were erected to draw attention to the site.

life dancing with skeletons. Other treasures in the museum include awe-inspiring altars from the 16th and 17th centuries, a collection of Renaissance and baroque chandeliers, and several curious 14th–17th-century tombstones. The museum also houses a **Silver Chamber** displaying exquisite ceremonial items from Tallinn's guilds.

Ruins on Harju Street

Making use of its wonderful acoustics, the church hosts **organ concerts** on weekend afternoons. A concert schedule is posted outside.

Freedom Square

Freedom Square (Vabaduse väljak), at the southern tip of the Old Town, has long been a place of symbolism: a statue of Peter the Great presided over it at the end of the tsarist period, and in Soviet times the square was used as a staging ground for military parades. Now the **Freedom Clock**, a frankly unimpressive monument installed in 2003, graces one end of the square with two narrow posts, one displaying the current time, the other the number of years since Estonia's first independence. Perhaps it's a testament to modern apathy that Estonians now use the square as a car park.

Architecture around the square reflects a definite style of the 1930s, because the area was built up during Estonia's pre-war economic boom. Buildings closest to the Old Town include several interesting galleries, whereas the ones opposite include a hotel, city offices, a casino and the Russian Drama Theatre. The late-19th-century **St John's Church** (Jaani kirik) dominates one side of the square.

BASTIONS AND MOATS

Mysteriously overlooked by most visitors, the scenic parks and paths that ring the east side of the Old Town offer a picture-perfect view of the town fortifications, not to mention a relaxing escape from the tourist crowds. The large, green area that starts at Freedom Square and extends nearly to Fat Margaret's Tower was once part of a system of bastions and moats that protected the town from attack. Now it's a favourite place for Tallinners of all ages to stroll, and is also the scene of a couple of highly educational sights related to Estonia's Soviet period.

Linda Hill monument

Harju Hill

Starting from Freedom Square you can ascend the stone steps and then the paths to the peak of **Harju Hill** (Harjumägi) for views of the surrounding city. Continuing towards the west, you soon reach Toompea Street. A detour to the bottom of this street will lead you to the **Museum of Occupation** at Toompea 8 (open Tues–Sun 11am–6pm; admission charge), a high-tech and dramatic introduction to the 1940–91 period, when Estonia was occupied first by the Soviet Union, then briefly by Nazi Germany, and again by the Soviets.

Linda Hill

Returning to Toompea Street, you can either cross through the lower **Hirve Park**, or climb back to the top of the street to visit the next rise, **Linda Hill** (Lindamägi). At the top stands a solemn monument to the mythical figure, Linda, whose husband Kalev, according to ancient lore, founded the town (*see page 30*). The statue predates

Toompark and the Schnelli Pond

World War II, but what's significant about it is that Tallinn residents adopted it during Soviet times as a kind of unsanctioned memorial to loved ones deported to Siberia. Since there would be no gravesite and no official memorial, relatives would lay flowers here, at considerable risk to themselves if they were caught. Even now the tradition continues, and a plaque that has been added reads 'To remember the ones who were taken away'.

Toompark

Past some buildings and a stadium on the other side of Falgi tee, the view becomes more scenic; Toompea Castle and the sharp cliffs below become visible from here. This is **Toompark**, whose paths and bridges surround **Schnelli Pond** (Snelli tiik), the only remaining part of the town's water-filled moat. A shack at the far end of the pond rents out pedal boats and rowing boats in summer and ice-skates in winter. Finally, a walk through **Tornide Square**, another green area just north of Nunne Street, offers the best possible view of Tallinn's medieval wall and towers. A break in the wall will take you back into the Lower Town.

KADRIORG

For Tallinn natives, the name 'Kadriorg' evokes images of affluence, nature and, most of all, tranquillity. This leafy neighbourhood of palaces, parks, ponds and villas just outside the city centre is the town's favourite place to stroll. By the same token, Kadriorg's sheer beauty and the extravagance of its architecture also make it an essential part of any Tallinn tour.

The area's name in Estonian (Kadri + *org*) means 'Catherine's Valley'. It owes its existence to Tsar Peter the Great, who in the early 18th century, soon after conquering Estonia in the Great Northern War, established a summer estate here, which he named in honour of his wife, Catherine I. From the beginning, the estate was open to the public, and townsfolk were free to wander among its forests and gardens. Eventually Kadriorg became residential. In the 19th century, wealthy Tallinn residents began to build grand, wooden villas in the area, and in the 1920s and 30s, chic, functionalist houses started to appear. Through the years, the area kept its upper-class appeal, and it remains one of Tallinn's most prestigious neighbourhoods.

With its mosaic of 18th–20th-century architecture, its pathways and statuary, Kadriorg has long been a captivating place to visit, and is the more so now because it is home to some of Tallinn's best art museums.

Kadriorg Palace

The jewel in the Kadriorg's crown is the lavish, baroque **Kadriorg Palace** (Kadrioru loss), built by Peter the Great in 1718. Designed by Niccolo Michetti, an Italian architect who also worked on the famous Peterhof near St Petersburg, the palace is laid out in Italian villa style – a main building flanked by two annexes. The tsar named it Ekaterinenthal, or Catherinenthal, in honour of his wife, and intended to use it as a summer residence, though in the end his family spent hardly any time here.

Kadriorg Palace

The palace is a stunning monument to imperial extravagance. Its two-storey **main hall**, decorated with rich stucco work and grandiose ceiling paintings, is considered one of the best examples of baroque design in Northern Europe. Behind the building, the carefully manicured, 18th-century-style **flower garden,** with its shooting fountains, is equally impressive.

As the building is itself a masterpiece, it is appropriate that it houses one of the nation's top art museums. The **Kadriorg Art Museum** (open May–Sept Tues–Sun 10am–5pm; Oct–Apr Wed–Sun 10am–5pm; admission charge) is the main home for Estonia's foreign art collection. Here precious paintings by Western European and Russian artists of the 16th–20th century are on display, as are prints, sculptures, superb works in metal and porcelain, and other creations.

While here, those interested in art should also visit the **Mikkel Museum** (open Wed–Sun 11am–6pm; admission charge), just across the street in what used to be the palace's

Kadriorg's main hall

kitchen building. Donated by a private collector, Johannes Mikkel, in 1994, the exquisite works include Flemish and Dutch paintings, Italian engravings and Chinese porcelain. The pride and joy of the collection is a set of four etchings by Rembrandt, one of which is a self-portrait.

Up the hill from the museums is the **Presidential Palace**, the office and residence of Estonia's head of state. Built in 1938, this palace is relatively modest compared to its neighbour, the Kardriorg Palace, which until then fulfilled this role. Though tourists aren't allowed inside, they may take photos of the exterior and of the guards marching out front.

Close to the palace is KUMU, the new home of the **Art Museum of Estonia** (open May–Sept Tues–Sun 11am–6pm, Thur until 9pm; Oct–Apr Wed–Sun 11am–6pm; admission charge), the country's largest, most sophisticated collection of Estonian art. The permanent exhibition covers the pre-World War II classics and the Soviet period, while temporary exhibitions showcase recent trends.

Kadriorg Park

The sprawling park that surrounds Kadriorg Palace encompasses open spaces, wooded areas, statues, benches, paths and ponds. In the early 18th century, Russian soldiers planted hundreds of chestnuts and other varieties of trees here, and areas of the park are now densely wooded.

By far the most dazzling of the park's sights is the large, rectangular **Swan Pond** adjacent to Weizenbergi Street, near the palace. The symmetrical pond with fountains and a beautiful, white gazebo at its centre could easily set the scene for a Tchaikovsky ballet. Here swans, ducks and pigeons all vie for the breadcrumbs that local children invariably throw, while their parents wander nearby, admiring the colourful flowerbeds that line the surrounding paths.

On the other side of the palace, a long, straight path leads towards the seashore, and to a magnificent statue of an angel, standing on a large stone pedestal, facing out to sea. This is the **Russalka** memorial, built to commemorate 177 men lost when the Russian warship, *Russalka,* sank en route from Tallinn to Helsinki in 1893. Russian-speaking couples traditionally lay flowers at the foot of this dramatic monument on their wedding day.

The Russalka memorial

Opposite the monument, slightly further down the coast, is the entrance to the **Song Festival Grounds** (Lauluväljak), home of Estonia's Song Festival, held every five years. It was here that the 'Singing Revolution' began *(see page 21)*, when hundreds of thousands of Estonians gathered in the summer of 1988 to sing traditional songs as a mass demonstration against Soviet dominance. The **Song Festival Arena**, with a distinctive, curving roof, was built in 1960 and is Tallinn's largest outdoor stage.

The port of Tallinn

THE PORT

The area around Tallinn's passenger port is fairly industrial and spread out, so it is not particularly tourist friendly. That said, visitors interested in ships and architecture will find some worthwhile sights.

The Estonian Maritime Museum operates two **museum ships** at the Lennusadam Harbour (Küti 15A). The first is the ***Lembit* submarine** (open daily 10am–7pm; admission charge), the only functioning submarine in the Baltics. Built in England in 1936 for the Estonian Navy, it later sailed under the Soviet flag. Visitors can climb inside to inspect the torpedo hatches, try out the crew's bunks and even look through the periscope. Built in 1914, the ***Suur Tõll* icebreaker** (open daily 10am–7pm; admission charge) kept the Baltic waterways clear for decades, and is the largest intact steam-powered icebreaker in the world. Tours of the engine rooms and crew rooms give visitors a glimpse of what maritime life was like almost a century ago.

The **Rotermanni Salt Storage** building at Ahtri 2 is an distinctive example of limestone architecture from 1908. It houses the **Museum of Estonian Architecture** (open June–Sept Wed–Fri noon–8pm, Sat–Sun 11am–6pm; Oct–May Wed–Sun 11am–6pm; admission charge) with rotating exhibitions. Students of architecture will also want to visit nearby **Linnahall**, a concert hall, ice rink and port. Built in 1980, this concrete monstrosity demonstrates the excesses of Soviet design.

OUTLYING AREAS

Pirita

Pirita, a district 10 minutes' drive north of the centre, easily qualifies as Tallinn's favourite playground. That's mainly thanks to the immensely popular **Pirita Beach**, a vast stretch of sand invariably packed with tanning bodies and frolicking children on any given summer day. The forested, mostly residential area also claims a number of other notable attractions, ranging from the captivatingly scenic to the ridiculously Soviet.

Squarely in the first category are the spectacular ruins of **St Bridget's Convent** (Pirita klooster; open June–Aug daily 9am–7pm; Apr–May, Sept daily 10am–6pm; Oct–Mar daily noon–4pm; admission charge). Founded by the Swedish Bridgettine Order in 1407, the convent operated here until

The gabled façade of St Bridget's Convent at Pirita

Ivan the Terrible's forces destroyed it in 1577. What remains are the convent's towering, gabled façade, the walls of its main building, several foundations, cellars and a cemetery.

Beyond the ruins, the tranquil **Pirita River** slowly winds its way through the district before emptying out into Tallinn Bay. Pedal boats, rowing boats and canoes can be rented by the hour from **Pirita Boat Rental** (Paadilaenutus; open May–Sept daily 10am–10pm), operating from the built-up embankment, downhill from the convent. A leisurely row or paddle is a perfect way to experience the lush, marshy beauty of the area.

In the Kloostrimetsa section of Pirita further inland, Tallinn's space-age-looking **TV Tower** (Teletorn; open daily 10am–1am; admission charge) dominates the skyline. At 314m (1,030ft), this is by far the tallest structure in town. Unforgettable views of the city and surrounding ports unfold

Pirita Beach is backed by pine trees

from its observation deck and restaurant at the 170m (560ft) level, and the coast of Finland can even be seen on a clear day. Just as amazing as the view, however, is the TV tower itself, an odd throwback to the Soviet 1980s both in its gargantuan structure and in its tacky interior design.

About 3km (2 miles) from Pirita is a plant-lover's paradise, the Tallinn Botanical Gardens (Tallinna Botaanikaaed; open Tues–Sun 11am–7pm; admission charge). More than 8,000 plant species can be found on 123 hectares (300 acres) of landscaped grounds. Greenhouses (open Tues–Sun 11am–4pm; admission charge) operate year-round, and have everything from rare varieties to houseplants.

Maarjamäe

This coastal hill just north of Kadriorg is a fascinating spot, particularly for visitors interested in World War II and Soviet history.

First and foremost, this is the site of the sprawling **Maarjamäe War Memorial**, an impossibly ugly and overbearing, cement-filled park that could only have been born of the Soviet 1960s and 70s. Its concrete avenues and abstract, iron sculptures were installed in 1975 to commemorate Soviet soldiers killed in Estonia during World War II. Many a semi-mandatory, enthusiastic Soviet rally was held at the now crumbling amphitheatre here. Ironically, the memorial is built on what had earlier been a German cemetery, now marked by the solemn crosses visible behind the complex.

Nearby stands the **Maarjamäe Palace** (Maarjamäe loss), a grand, pseudo-Gothic manor built by Count Orlov-Davidov in 1874. Originally used as summer home, the 'palace' changed hands several times through the years, serving as a Dutch consul's residence, a prestigious hotel, an aviation school and even a Soviet army barracks. The building now

Knitting at the Estonian Open Air Museum in Rocca al Mare

houses a branch of the **Estonian History Museum** (open Mar–Oct Wed–Sun 11am–6pm; Nov–Feb Wed–Sun 10am–5pm; admission charge), which chronicles the 19th and 20th centuries. Especially interesting are its displays on Estonia's first period of independence and World War II.

Rocca al Mare

Once a private, seaside estate, this forested park on the western edge of Kopli Bay is now home to one of Tallinn's most popular tourist attractions, the **Estonian Open Air Museum** (Eesti Vabaõhumuuseum; open May–Oct daily 10am–8pm, houses and pub until 6pm; Nov–Apr daily 10am–5pm; admission charge). Dozens of thatch-roofed 18th–20th century farmhouses, barns, windmills and watermills combine to give a vivid impression of what Estonian village life must have been like in times past. This is far from a static museum – characters dressed in period costume drive horse carts through the park, others perform chores in the various buildings while visitors look on. One of the mandatory stops here is the Kolu Tavern, famous for its traditional Estonian pea soup.

Visitors should set aside at least half a day to tour the park properly. Those who have children with them should also note that both the **Tallinn Zoo** and the city's largest amusement park, the **Rocca al Mare Tivoli**, are in the same part of town.

EXCURSIONS

A day trip from Tallinn will allow you to experience the rugged splendour of Estonia's countryside or explore one of the nation's other notable cities, each of which has a history and spirit quite different from those in the capital. For visitors with more time on their hands, hiring a car is a good way to see the country. That said, it is not essential; convenient buses connect Tallinn to the cities mentioned here, and for the more out-of-the-way locations organised tours are available.

Lahemaa National Park

Along the northern coast about an hour's drive east of Tallinn lies Estonia's largest nature reserve, **Lahemaa National Park** (Lahemaa rahruspark), a perfect antidote to urban tourism. The 725 sq km (280 sq mile) park encompasses vast areas of forest,

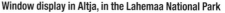

Window display in Altja, in the Lahemaa National Park

jagged seashores, wetlands and several historic villages as well as some stunning 17th–18th-century manor houses.

Your first stop should be **Palmse Manor**, the most striking manor house in the country. Completed in 1740, it was home to the von der Pahlen family until 1919 when a land reform law nationalised the manorial holdings and divided them among local peasants. The house then served as a convalescent home and later a Soviet pioneer camp, but it has since been renovated and now operates as a museum (open May–Sept daily 10am–7pm; Oct–Apr daily 10am–5pm; admission charge). Visitors are welcome to stroll the manor grounds where they'll find a peaceful swan pond and landscaped gardens.

The manor also serves as Lahemaa's **Visitor Centre** (open May–Aug daily 9am–7pm; Sept daily 9am–5pm; Oct–Apr Mon–Fri 9am–5pm). Here you'll find maps and information on the park's sights and nature walks.

The striking Palmse Manor

Not far away is another impressive manor house, **Sagadi Manor**. It was built in 1749, but renovated at the end of that century in a classicist style. Like Palmse, it's now open to visitors, and one of its renovated outbuildings houses a forestry museum.

The boulder-strewn coastline

Lahemaa's other attractions include several hamlets, such as **Altja**, a lovely Estonian fishing village. The old wooden buildings here were restored in the 1970s, and the village has since become a popular local tourist spot. Here you'll find a 19th-century inn, a traditional village swing and several paths along the coast.

Another coastal village, **Käsmu**, is less typical. This one has a decidedly affluent look as a result of its residents' salt-smuggling activities in the 19th century. In the 1920s, when Finland imposed prohibition, the economic focus here naturally shifted to alcohol. Apart from the houses of wealthy sea captains, Käsmu is known for its **Maritime Museum** (free), housed in what was once a school of navigation.

Like Käsmu, the village of **Viinistu** also profited from alcohol smuggling, but what puts it on the map nowadays is something else entirely. This village of just 150 people is home to the **Viinistu Art Museum** (open daily 11am–6pm; admission charge), which has the largest private art collection in Estonia. The 19th and 20th century Estonian paintings on display easily rival those of the state-owned museums in Tallinn. This anomaly is thanks to one former resident who, as a child, fled with his family to Sweden during World War II. After making his fortune as manager of the pop group Abba, he returned to Viinistu, eventually converting a Soviet-era fish collective into this art centre. Apart from the museum, the village has a respectable tavern and a small trail that follows its coastline.

Jägala Waterfall

On the way to Lahemaa, visitors can take a small detour north from the Narva Highway to the village of Jägala-Joa, home to one of Estonia's best-known beauty spots, the **Jägala Waterfall**. About 8m (26ft) high and at times as much as 70m (230ft) wide, the waterfall is given its uniquely spectacular look by the way the river pours over the edge of a perfectly flat limestone shelf. The exposed cliff face reveals more layers of limestone, a geological feature for which northern Estonia is famous. Through the centuries, the waterfall has cut a gorge that's 300m (980ft) long and 12–14m (39–46ft) deep.

The Jägala Waterfall

Naissaar

Anyone interested in military history or nature – and who doesn't mind a bit of hiking – should consider a day trip to the island of Naissaar, about 10km (6 miles) from the coast of Tallinn. Since the late 1990s most of the island has been a nature reserve, but for nearly 50 years it was a closed Soviet naval base. Ironically, its name literally means 'women's island', a name

Because the Baltic Sea is virtually enclosed by land it is environmentally extremely sensitive. It takes around 35 years for all of the water in the sea to be replaced by water from the ocean beyond. If any pollutants enter the water, they will stay there for two or three decades, by which time they may have severely damaged the area's ecosystems.

thought to originate from an 11th-century legend of the island's beautiful maidens.

The base's main function was the manufacture of **sea mines**, the casings of which now litter the island. De-mining operations removed over 5,000 of the explosive devices before the island was opened to tourists in 1998, but this was by no means all of them and it's essential to stay on established trails and closely follow rules about where to camp.

The island is 11km (7 miles) long and 4km (2½ miles) wide and many visitors prefer organised tours such as the one offered by Naissaare Reisid (tel: 6398 000). The island can otherwise be explored on foot or by bicycle. Naissaar's **Nature Park Centre**, uphill from the dock, should be your first stop. Here you'll find information, coffee and maps of the island's two major **trails**. Animals you might spot include deer, fox, rabbits and even moose. In summer, the beautiful, pink *Rosa rugosa* blooms all over the island, and there are also a number of quiet, sandy beaches to explore. The island's only village, **Männiku**, is about 20 minutes' walk from the port and has an old-fashioned saloon, guest-house and a railway station.

Military sights around the island include the abandoned **mine factory**, the so-called **Fairy Village**, which is a ghost town that once housed Soviet military personnel, and **Bunker 10B**, the remains of concrete bunkers. Trails also take visitors to the island's two **lighthouses**, and past **cemeteries** where English and French soldiers from the Crimean War are buried.

A trip to the island requires planning. The only regular ferry, the *Monica*, makes the trip from Tallinn's Pirita Harbour once in the morning and returns once in the late afternoon. It operates only in summer, and only from Wednesday to Sunday. Phone 1182 for exact times and prices.

Pärnu

Each year, when the seasons change and the weather finally starts to turn warm, Estonians like to abandon their dreary offices and schoolrooms and head off to Pärnu, their 'summer capital', on a coastal inlet 129km (80 miles) south of Tallinn. This quiet resort town of about 46,000 is known for its leafy parks, health spas, quaint town centre and, most of all, its long stretch of white sandy beach.

Though Pärnu is more than 750 years old and has seen numerous changes of empire, its most relevant history starts in 1838 when the town's first health spa was established. Thanks to the curative properties of the town's mud treatments, relatively warm weather and sea air, Pärnu grew into a popular spa destination and by the end of the 19th century had developed into one of the most prominent health resorts in the Russian empire. Pärnu's status as a resort continued even during the turbulent 20th century. In the post-Soviet era, investment and much-needed income from Finnish clients helped bring its resort industry back up to date. Now it can claim seven spa hotels offering everything from plastic surgery to water slides.

When most travellers first arrive in Pärnu, they find themselves in the historic downtown area, the centrepiece of which is **Rüütli Street**. This long, pedestrian walkway and the few streets that surround it are home to the town's most exclusive shops and a hotchpotch of intriguing buildings from the 17th to the 20th century. The most impressive of these landmarks are the imposing **Eliisabeti Church**, from 1747, the dazzling Orthodox **Ekateriina Church** from 1768, and the mid-17th-century **Almshouse** (Seegi maja), which now operates as a restaurant. Another notable 17th-century structure, the **Tallinn Gate** (Tallinna väravad), marks what used to be the road to Tallinn before the Pärnu River was finally spanned in 1938. Pärnu's oldest building is the **Red Tower** (Punane torn), a squat, 15th-century tower that once

Pärnu Town Hall and, in the distance, the spires of Ekateriina Church

guarded the edge of town. The tower, which is now painted white, is hidden in an alley adjacent to Hommiku Street.

Just outside the downtown area is **Koidula Park**, named after Lydia Koidula (1843–86), the matriarch of Estonian poetry. Colourful flowerbeds, a fountain and several paths make this an excellent place to relax or stroll. On the streets nearby you can find several examples of old, wooden villas and functionalist houses from the pre-war period.

A few minutes' walk south brings you to Pärnu's true centre of gravity – the beach. Cafés, volleyball nets, ice-cream vendors, lifeguards and all the other trappings of a typical, world-class beach can be found here. The only things lacking are crashing waves and sharks. When you tire of bronzing yourself on the sand, you can take time to see the area's treasures. The **Beach House** (Rannahoone), with a distinctive, mushroom-shaped balcony, dates from 1939 and is a wonderful example of functionalism. The same can be said of the striking **Beach Hotel** (Rannahotell) nearby, completed in 1937. The neoclassical **Pärnu Mud Bath** building (Pärnu Mudaravila), with a dome-shaped roof and circular garden, has become a symbol of the town, as has the art nouveau mansion, **Ammende Villa**, slightly further away down Mere Puiestee.

Also adjacent to the beach is the **Beach Park** (Rannapark), established in 1882. You can slowly meander through the park and contemplate the scenery, or hire a pair of roller skates at the beach and rocket along its many paved paths.

Tartu

Its nickname is 'the city of good thoughts', but a better name for Tartu, a minor metropolis 189km (118 miles) southeast of Tallinn, might be 'the city of good ideas'. Tartu is Estonia's intellectual capital, home not only to the nation's largest and most prestigious educational institution, Tartu University, but also to several colleges, research centres and the nation's supreme court.

The atmosphere here is decidedly different from that in Tallinn – less rushed, more contemplative and, thanks to its student population, visibly younger. With 101,000 inhabitants, this is Estonia's second-largest city, but Tartu is still small enough to lack the annoyances found in urban areas. At the same time it has a number of cafés, parks, museums and historic sites that are just as interesting as any you could find in the capital.

As in Tallinn, the heart of Tartu is its **Old Town**, where the city's most striking ar-

Oscar and Eduard Wilde
(see page 77)

chitecture is concentrated. Unlike Tallinn, though, Tartu's Old Town no longer has a medieval look – constant wars during the 17th century and the Great Fire of 1775 mean that most of what you see here was built in the late 18th and 19th centuries. Your first Old Town destination should be **Town Hall Square** (Raekoja plats), the centre of Tartu from time immemorial, and home to the city's helpful **Tourist Information** office. The **Town Hall** (Raekoda) presiding over the top of the square is actually the third town hall built in this spot. It was opened in 1786 and its design reflects a mixture of early classicism, baroque and rococo. As in older times, the building serves as the city's administrative centre. The

Kissing Students and onlookers

mischievous fountain directly in front of the Town Hall, **Kissing Students**, is a recent installation, but has already become a favourite symbol of the town.

Further down the square is Tartu's Leaning Tower of Pisa, the **Kivisilla Art Gallery** (open Wed–Sun, 11am–6pm; admission charge), which tilts bizarrely to the left due to the soft riverbank mud on which it stands. The nearby **arched bridge** over the Emajõgi River replaced the 18th-century stone bridge that was destroyed in 1944. Taking a daring walk over the arched bridge's top rail has become a student tradition.

Just off the square from the Town Hall you'll find one of the most outstanding examples of neoclassical architecture in Estonia, the **Tartu University Main Building** (open Mon–Fri 11am–5pm; admission charge). The Swedish King Gustav Adolph established Tartu University in 1632, and this structure was completed in 1809. The building houses an impressive concert hall, an art museum whose collection of antiquities includes a 4,000-year-old Egyptian mummy, and a Student Lock-up, where students were incarcerated for bad conduct. Not far away is **St John's Church** (Jaani Kirik), whick dates back to the late 12th century. The church has undergone years of renovation and should now be open to the public.

A short climb up **Toome Hill** (Toomemägi) brings you to the towering brick ruins of **Dome Cathedral**. Built in the

13th century, the cathedral served as the centre of a regional bishopric prior to the Reformation. Fire destroyed it in 1624. A restored section of the cathedral was once used as the university's library, but it now houses the extensive **Museum of Tartu University History** (open Wed–Sun 11am–5pm; admission charge), which displays old lab equipment, photos and a 13th-century celestial globe. Another crest of the hill is home to Tartu's **Old Observatory**, which began operation in 1810 and is now a museum.

Finally, no visit to Tartu would be complete without a stop at **Wilde**, an extravagantly decorated Irish pub, bookshop and bakery known and loved throughout Estonia. A statue in front of the pub depicts a chance meeting of Oscar Wilde (1854–1900) and the Estonian writer Eduard Wilde (1865–1933) on a park bench – a somewhat impish creation considering how doubtful it is that the two ever met.

Tartu University

Haapsalu

People from all over the world come looking for cures from Haapsalu's sea mud. News of its efficacy was spread by Carl Abraham Hunnius, a military doctor, who founded the first mud treatment centre here in 1825. It wasn't long before the fashionable folk of St Petersburg's were making their way to Haapsalu.

This seaside town 101km (63 miles) southwest of Tallinn gives an insight into small-town life in Estonia. Early 20th-century wooden houses dominate Haapsalu's central neighbourhoods, many of its narrow streets have never been paved, and its residents seem to amble about in a particularly unhurried manner. At the same time, this resort town, which competes with Pärnu for the title of having the nation's most therapeutic mud, is home to enough historic curiosities to make a trip here worthwhile for anyone with a day to spare.

Haapsalu's best-known attraction is the late 13th-century **Episcopal Castle** that dominates the town centre. The castle served as both religious outpost and military fortress until Peter the Great conquered it at the beginning of the 18th century. Though it mostly lies in ruins, much of the structure is still intact and visitors are free to stroll through its grassy courtyard and examine its remaining walls and old cannons. In summer one section operates as a **museum** (open Tues–Sun 10am–6pm; admission charge) chronicling the town's history. When the museum is open, visitors can also pay to climb the castle's **watchtower** from where there's a magnificent view.

One part of the castle that's not in ruins is the **Haapsalu Dome Church**, whose beautiful interior you can see if you tour the castle's museum. One of the church's windows is central to the town's favourite legend, 'The White Lady of Haapsalu'. The ghostly figure of a woman, who was supposedly immured in the castle walls, is said to appear on the window on moonlit nights in August. An annual White Lady Days Festival is named after the legend.

Not far from here is the town's seaside **promenade**, a good place for a stroll. Here you'll see a grand-looking, wooden **Resort Hall** (Kuursaal), which operates as a restaurant in summer. Next to it is a **stone bench** that, with the help of modern technology, talks and plays classical music. This is a monument to the composer Pyotr Tchaikovsky, who supposedly got the inspiration for *Swan Lake* while resting in Haapsalu.

Rail enthusiasts should head to the **Estonian Railway Museum** (open Wed–Sun 10am–6pm; admission charge). Built into Haapsalu's romantic, early 20th-century railway station, the small museum displays a replica stationmaster's room, passenger's waiting room and a number of tools and uniforms. Outside on the tracks is a collection of locomotives and engines from the 1940s and 50s.

Locomotive at the Estonian Railway Museum

WHAT TO DO

ENTERTAINMENT

During the height of the tourist season, live, outdoor entertainment isn't just easy to find in Tallinn, it's nearly impossible to escape. Every kind of music, from traditional Estonian folk to Scottish bagpipes, echoes through the air as small, seemingly impromptu concerts erupt on squares and street corners of the Old Town.

The most uniquely Estonian events are those involving national song and dance. Generally these folk performances are held only when specific festivals are scheduled, but if you happen to see groups of women wearing brightly striped village skirts, follow them to their concert and you'll be rewarded with beautiful, rural music traditions that go back hundreds of years.

Classical Music, Opera and Ballet

Estonia's national concert organiser, Eesti Kontsert, acts as a kind of one-stop-shop for Tallinn's classical performances. The company sells tickets for a whole spectrum of classical entertainment from its box office in the **Estonia Theatre** (Estonia pst. 4, tel: 6147 760; open daily noon–7pm). Opera tickets are sold in another part of the same building. Larger classical events take place in the theatre itself, while

In summer you'll find a classical concert or dance performance in Tallinn just about every night of the week. For an up-to-date list of what's happening on the cultural front, check the city tourist office's homepage (<www.tourism.tallinn.ee>).

Guitar Safari, a cellar bar for rock lovers

medieval churches, guild halls and towers provide interesting venues for the smaller performances. To see what events are coming up, check the 'Infopunkt' billboards posted around the Old Town (attached to street maps).

For a change from the usual *Swan Lake* and *La Traviata*, buy tickets to any show given by Tallinn's early music ensemble, **Hortus Musicus**, whose repertoire of baroque and Renaissance music fits in well with the city's historic ambience. **Organ Concerts**, held every Saturday and Sunday afternoon in St Nicholas's Church (Niguliste 3), offer a more casual, classical performance option. Concert times are posted outside the church.

Pop and Rock Music

The city's small but lively band scene mainly revolves around its bars and clubs *(see page 84)*, but every so often stand-alone concerts take place, usually in connection with some kind of music festival. Additionally, major international stars occasionally visit Tallinn when their current tour brings them to this part of Europe. In both cases, advertisements all around the city will make sure you know what's going on.

To see what the events are before you make your trip, check the Piletilevi ticket agency's website <www.piletilevi.ee>, which also gives you information about tickets and lets you book them online.

Cinema

Cinema is an easy entertainment option in Tallinn as films are nearly always shown in their original language, with Estonian subtitles. The 11-screen Coca-Cola Plaza (Hobujaama 5) screens mainly Hollywood fare, while the Sõprus (Vana-Posti 8) concentrates on art-house films. Phone 1182 for all show times and information in English.

NIGHTLIFE

There's absolutely no better way to relax in Tallinn than to sit in an outdoor café, beer in hand, watching the world slowly meander past. When the day gets late, however, most people like to head for more social surroundings. Fortunately, the city has a wide spectrum of nightlife to explore – everything from quiet, sophisticated lounges to pulsing dance clubs.

Hell Hunt has a good atmosphere

Like everything else in Tallinn, most of the nightlife is squeezed into a few Old Town streets, giving rise to the custom of frequent bar-hopping. Since the bars are literally only a few paces apart, locals (and savvy visitors) will often change locations after every single drink, exploring all the options until they finally find the place they want to settle in.

Bars and pubs are easy to find in the Old Town – just follow the crowds and the noise. Beware, though, that annoying groups of British stag weekenders (bachelor partiers) have infiltrated many of the central pubs, so the saner crowds tend to go elsewhere. **Molly Malone's** (Mündi 2, tel: 6313 016) on the square is still a safe bet and has good live music most weekends. **Hell Hunt** (Pikk 39, tel: 6818 333) has a good atmosphere and its own brand of beer. Local flavour can be found in the crowded **Karja-Kelder** (Väike-Karja 1, tel: 6441 008).

For more cosmopolitan, lounge-type surroundings, **Lounge 8** (Vana-Posti 8, tel: 6274 770) and **Pegasus** (Harju 1, tel: 6314 040) are both good choices. Cosy wine bars have also become fashionable. Two highly recommended wine bars are **Kolme Näoga Mees** (Kuninga 1, tel: 6484 261) and **Gloria Veinikelder** (Müürivahe 2, tel: 6448 846).

Tallinn is home to an active, local band scene, and many of the larger bars and pubs offer live music on weekends. A couple of these, such as **Von Krahli Baar** (Rataskaevu 10, tel: 6269 096) and the cop-themed **Scotland Yard** (Mere pst. 6e, tel: 6535 190), build much of their business on live performance. The free mini-magazine *Heat*, distributed in bars, has the most complete schedule of who is playing where. Ask a local which of the bands are their favourites.

Nightclubs are also easy to find, but hard to recommend. Crowds are fickle, so what could be full of life on one night could be desolate the next. One that's always enormously popular, however, is the huge, central **Club Hollywood** (Vana-Posti 8, tel: 6274 770), which draws a young crowd. The scene at nearby **Club Privé** (Harju 6, tel: 6310 545) is more exclusive and mature.

SHOPPING

The explosive growth in Tallinn's retail sector over the past few years means you'll have absolutely no trouble stuffing your suitcase with gifts, souvenirs and other goodies. More shops and boutiques blossom with each new tourist season, and several shopping malls – a rare species until recently – now crowd the downtown area. What's more, the credit card has become king; thanks to the demands of technology-loving Estonian shoppers, all but the smallest locations will now happily accept your plastic.

Despite these huge improvements in the shopping culture, however, Estonia is still a fairly secluded market,

Traditional woollens at the 'Wall of Sweaters' knitwear market

which means that not everything here is a bargain. For example, foreign-manufactured clothes can actually cost more in Tallinn than in relatively rich Scandinavia. Likewise, electronics are almost always more expensive here than in Western countries. The upshot is that you can't assume that things are cheaper here, and comparing prices to what you would pay at home is crucial if you want to avoid spending blunders.

Nevertheless, with some types of products, you can almost always find good value. Anything made locally, particularly handicrafts, art and Estonian-produced fashion, is a safe bet. Additionally, alcohol and cigarettes are typically a steal here because Estonia doesn't tax these items nearly as much as Western countries do. This explains why Finnish beer is so much cheaper in Estonia than in Finland, and why the ferry back to Helsinki is always crowded with bleary-eyed karaoke stars.

Where to Shop

> Market vendors may give you a small discount for buying in volume, but generally they don't barter. The price they quote is what they expect to get.

Without doubt, the Old Town holds the most promise for the intrepid souvenir hunter. This area has by far the highest concentration of shops specialising in linen, glass, ceramics, knitwear and other locally made wares. It also abounds with larger, more general *suveniir* stores. All the items they sell are typical of Estonia, plus T-shirts, postcards and the like. Similarly, establishments offering antiques, art and traditional handicrafts line just about every street, especially those nearest Town Hall Square. In short, almost anywhere you are in the Old Town, you'll be able to find shopping within a few metres.

Outdoor markets, while not actually common in Tallinn, present the most interesting shopping experience. First and foremost is the much-loved **knitwear market** along the old city wall on Müürivahe Street, near the Viru Gates. Since it doesn't have an official name, most foreigners simply refer to it as the **Wall of Sweaters**. Here local women sell just about every kind of knitted item you can imagine, with a better variation in styles than in most shops. A similar, but less spectacular craft market operates nearby on Mere Puiestee, just north of Vana-Viru Street. In summer, temporary markets also appear from week to week on or near Town Hall Square, where there is an enchanting **Christmas Market**.

An equally fascinating place to pick up a gift or two is the **Katariina Guild**, in St Catherine's Passage (Katariina käik), which runs from the Wall of Sweaters to Vene Street. In this string of small workshops, visitors can watch craftswomen at work creating quilts, ceramics, glass items, jewellery, hats and hand-painted silk. While the artists use time-honoured methods, their products are usually modern, even avant-garde.

The more traditional Estonian handicraft items are available in any souvenir shop, but the most authentic and interesting are sold by **Eesti Käsitöö** (Estonian Handicraft), which operates shops on Müürivahe 17, Kuninga 1, and Viru 1 (in the Demini shopping centre). Here you can find everything from dolls and wooden toys to entire Estonian folk costumes.

Shoppers looking for everyday fashions and other non-souvenir items will find the best selection in large department stores and malls outside the Old Town. The most notable of these are the **Viru Centre** and the attached **Kaubamaja** department store, both located in central Tallinn next to Viru Square. Tallinn's branch of **Stockmann**, the esteemed Finnish department store, is a short walk from there at Liivalaia 53. Other good shopping centres, such as the **Kristiine Centre** and the **Ülemiste Centre**, can be reached by taxi.

Felt hats

What to Buy

Handicrafts, in all shapes and forms, are still the undisputed rulers of the city's souvenir world, thanks to modern Estonia's strong connection to its rural past. **Knitted items**, such as woollen jumpers, mittens, gloves, socks and hats, top the list in popularity. Most of the knitwear is created in typical Estonian or Nordic patterns. A particularly fun variation sold here is a ridiculously long woollen cap, the drooping end of which is supposed to be tied around the neck like a scarf. Almost as common as knitwear is **linen**, which has been produced here since medieval times. A huge variety of linen articles is available, ranging from tablecloths to dresses.

Anything made of **carved wood**, particularly the fragrant juniper, is also a popular Estonian souvenir. Toys, dolls, beer mugs, butter knives and countless other wooden handicrafts sold in the shops make excellent and inexpensive gifts.

Though it actually comes from Lithuania and Poland, **amber** has become a pan-Baltic souvenir, and many visitors feel obliged to pick up at least one piece of amber jewellery when visiting Tallinn. Apart from its well-known light-caramel colour, it can also be found in white, green and a deep brown.

Baltic speciality

Antiques of all sorts are widely sold throughout the Old Town. Antique furniture, gramophones, Russian icons and the like are available, though buyers should be aware of the restrictions on exporting items made before 1945 *(see page 112)*. Even for non-collectors, browsing one of the low-end antique shops can be an adventure as they're typically packed with unique **Soviet-era trinkets**. The long list of

USSR flotsam available in Tallinn includes busts of Lenin, patriotic posters, postcards and pins, and military items ranging from Red Army officers' hats to night-vision scopes.

Tallinn is also an excellent place to find **gifts** such as jewellery and beautiful, hand-painted silk scarves. Offbeat and sometimes bizarre creations in ceramics and glass are always fun to inspect.

Tallinn's own liqueur

One souvenir that says 'Tallinn' like no other is **Vana Tallinn liqueur**, available in any alcohol shop for a modest price. The sweet, dark liquid can be sipped as-is from a shot glass or, better still, added to coffee or ice cream. Bottles of Vana Tallinn are often sold in linen satchels, making them very presentable as gifts. Finally, just as sweet as the liqueur but far less hazardous are **chocolates** made by Tallinn's famous Kalev confectionery company. Large boxes of assorted chocolates with photos or etchings of Tallinn make good mementos.

SPORTS

Given Estonia's cold climate, it's natural that the favourite sports here are the indoor and winter varieties.

Basketball has long been the spectator sport of choice in Estonia. Tallinn's Kalev is the most recognised of the handful of teams based around the country. The national team plays tournaments in the Saku Suurhall (Paldiski mnt. 104B, tel: 6600 200). Though the Estonian team doesn't excel compared to its neighbours, **football** is fast catching up to basket-ball in popularity. Major games are held in the A. Le Coq Arena (Asula 4c, tel: 6279 940). On some weekends, weather permitting, **horse racing** take place in the Hipodroom (Paldiski mnt. 50, tel: 6771 677).

Fans who want to watch their home team's rugby or football match on satellite TV should head to the Old Town pubs such as Nimeta (Suur-Karja 4, tel: 6411 515), O'Malleys (Viru 24, tel: 6313 136) or Hell Hunt (Pikk 39, tel: 6818 333), all of which have large screens and plenty of beer and snacks.

Tallinn's one and only **golf course** is the 18-hole Niitvälja Golf (tel: 6780 110), located in Niitvälja, about 30 minutes from town. **Squash** players can satisfy their needs at Metro Squash (Tondi 17, tel: 6556 392), which will also rent equipment. A few **tennis** clubs in Tallinn are also visitor-friendly. Good choices are the Rocca-al-Mare Onistar Tennis Centre (Haabersti 5, tel: 6600 520), and the Kalevi Tenniseklubi (Herne 28, tel: 6459 229).

Those who like to get wet can try their hand at **windsurfing**. Hawaii Express (Regati 1, tel: 6398 508) holds weekly lessons for beginners at Pirita Beach. For a simple **swim** any time of year, Club 26 (Liivalaia 33, 6315 585) is a good option. Located on the 26th floor of the Olümpia Hotel, it offers the pool with the best view in town.

In winter, **ice-skating** is a popular activity. You can head to indoor rinks like the one in the Linnahall Ice Hall (Mere pst. 20, tel: 6412 266) or, if it's cold enough, try the Schnelli Pond, in the small park between the Old Town and the railway station.

In Estonia skiing is second nature. Every February thousands set out on the gruelling 60-km (37-mile) Tartu Marathon. The cross-country race is part of the international Worldloppet series, and attracts competitors from around the world.

Toomas the Train

CHILDREN

Tallinn doesn't offer too many obvious activities for children, but with a little strategic planning, you should have no trouble keeping the smile on any young face.

The most fun way to tour the Old Town in summer is hitching a ride on **Toomas the Train**. The red-and-black electric trackless train departs from Vana-Turg Street (near Olde Hansa restaurant) and makes a 20-minute circuit through the cobblestone streets. The big, white **bicycle taxis** operating in the centre also provide an amusing option for getting around.

Child-friendly **museums** include the Doll Museum (Kotzebue 16, tel: 6413 491), filled with teddy bears, dolls and other toys, and the Tallinn Science and Technology Centre (Põhja pst. 29, tel: 7152 650), where young audiences are dazzled with lightning displays and hands-on activities such as making giant soap bubbles. The Kalev Confectionery Museum (Pikk 16) reveals the secrets of making chocolate.

The **Estonian Puppet Theatre** (Lai 1, tel: 6679 550) stages short performances for tots. The language is Estonian, but the colourful action is universal. Very young children can also be entertained at special indoor **play centres** such as the Jõmmi mängutuba (Narva mnt. 31, tel: 6558 358) or Riki-Tiki (Pärnu mnt. 59, tel: 6461 025). These offer ball pools, trampolines and tiny climbing walls, as well as crafts and organised entertainment. Here parents typically attend, whereas at the Reds play centres in the Kristiine Keskus and Ülemiste Keskus shopping malls your children will be watched over while you shop.

The **Tallinn Zoo** (Paldiski mnt. 145, tel: 6943 300) never fails to enthral young visitors. More than 350 species of animals, including wolves, tigers, bears, elephants and lynx, make their home here. An essential stop is the zoo's popular Tropical House, which simulates rainforest conditions.

Older children will want to head out to the **FK Centre** (Paldiski mnt. 229a, tel: 6870 101) where they can engage in a laser shoot-out or live out their Formula-1 fantasies on the high-speed, motorised go-cart track. More types of fast-paced fun can be found at the **Rocca al Mare Tivoli** (Paldiski mnt. 100, tel: 6560 110; open mid-May–Aug), which operates 18 different thrill rides and dozens of carnival games.

Kite-flying on Pirita Beach

When the weather is decent, however, there are no more relaxing family activities than playing on Pirita Beach, renting rowing boats on the nearby Pirita River, or strolling through the Kadriorg district and feeding the ducks at the swan pond.

Calendar of Events

Tallinn hosts a number of festivals throughout the year, most of them centred on music and dance performances or designed to showcase the city's medieval past. In this extreme climate, events are carefully scheduled to take account of the season, though jazz festivals, dance festivals and classical concert cycles might happen at any time of year. Visitors may also be interested in major festivals going on in nearby towns. Big draws are the popular Viljandi Folk Festival, hosted in late July in the historic, southern town of Viljandi, and the Watergate water festival in Pärnu, also in July

1 January New Year's fireworks on Harju Hill, gathering in Town Hall Square.

January–February OpeNBaroque: long-standing series of concerts centred on baroque and other early musical styles (late January or early February).

April Jazzkaar: international jazz festival, featuring world-class performers from Estonia and abroad (late April).

May–June Grillfest: casual, two-day event involving barbecues, games and rock music (weekend and location vary).

June Old Town Days Festival: entertaining mix of medieval tournaments, markets and concerts all over the Old Town (first week of June).

July Beer Summer: the season's largest outdoor party. Five days of beer tasting, concerts by Estonia's top bands, carnival rides and games for children (early July).

July–August International Organ Festival (late July or early August).

August August Dance: modern dance performances by the most cutting-edge groups from Estonia and abroad.

November–December Black Nights Film Festival: International feature films, with sub-festivals for student films, children's films and animation (two weeks, beginning late November or early December).

December Christmas Jazz, an event similar to Jazzkaar in April but smaller in scale (early December). Christmas Market in Town Hall Square (throughout the month).

EATING OUT

With such a variety of dining options available in Tallinn – from romantic cellar cafés to exotic ethnic restaurants – eating out can be every bit as exciting as exploring the medieval capital itself. The Old Town in particular is so full of competing establishments that many have taken to having staff, sometimes in medieval or theme costumes, patrolling the streets to lure in would-be customers with leaflets and coupons.

Eating out is a relative bargain. Full meals in restaurants can easily be found for as little as €8–10 per person. Even the most exclusive establishments will charge only around €20 for a main course. Beware, however, of the outdoor cafés along Viru Street and on Town Hall Square, many of

Al fresco on Town Hall Square

which fall under the 'tourist trap' classification, with their high prices, slow service and mediocre food.

Meal Times

Breakfast is typically served between 7 and 10am on week-days, and as late as noon on weekends. Restaurants are open for lunch at 11am or noon for the odd early customer, though lunch breaks peak between 1 and 2pm. Dinner crowds fill restaurants between 6.30 and 8pm on weekdays, shifting to about an hour later on Friday and Saturday evenings. Late diners should note that restaurants stop serving food around 10 or 11pm, but some pubs in the Old Town will keep their kitchens open until midnight or later.

Breakfast

Nearly all hotels include breakfast in the price of the room. Depending on the establishment, this could be anything from a bread roll with cheese and a cup of coffee to an extensive breakfast buffet with five types of juice. The Estonian breakfast differs little from its typical continental European counterpart; eggs, sausage, muesli, cornflakes and yoghurt are the mainstays.

Local additions include the ever-popular porridge, as well as dark bread and slices of tomato, cucumber and cheese for making sandwiches. Chunks of herring are often available in many breakfast buffets.

Outside the hotels, a full breakfast is hard to find. The idea of eating breakfast out hasn't caught on in Estonia, and few restaurants open before 11am. One notable exception is **Pegasus** (Harju 1, tel: 6314 040), which opens at 8am week-days and offers a full breakfast menu, bagels included.

An excellent alternative for anyone who wants to get an early bite is to visit one of the many bakeries in the town centre and Old Town. These usually open at 7 or 8am, and serve a huge variety of fresh pastries, croissants and cakes, along with coffee and tea. Most have a few small tables available for customers who want to enjoy their pastries on the spot. In the Old Town, these bakeries can be recognised by the traditional, pretzel-shaped signs hanging outside, and of course by irresistibly sugary, baking aromas wafting out into the street. In case those directions are too vague, try **Balti-Sepik** (Suur-Karja 3) or **Otto Pagariäri** (Pikk 35). The town's oldest bakery/café, **Maiasmokk** (Pikk 16, tel: 6464 066), is worth visiting for its old-fashioned décor alone.

Traditional Cuisine

Sampling the local fare is a must when visiting Tallinn, but it's important to make the distinction between 'traditional Estonian cuisine' and what Estonians actually eat these days.

The former developed through centuries of Estonian village life, though it also shows clear Germanic and Scandinavian influences. Many of these dishes are, frankly, not for the faint hearted. One quintessentially Estonian item is *sült*, a jellied meat dish made by slowly reducing pork bones (and sometimes hooves and heads). It is served cold, with a touch of mustard or horseradish. Other traditional items include marinated eel, Baltic sprats and *mulgikapsad* (a kind of sauerkraut stew with pork). Pea soup with ham gets worked into the equation when the weather turns cold, and *verivorst* (blood sausage) is a Christmas favourite.

> **'Our favourite spice is salt. When we're feeling really wild, we'll use a dash of pepper.'**
> **– A local quip about the simplicity of Estonian cuisine.**

Trying out these time-honoured dishes will definitely be an experience to remember, but these are only part of the story. Restaurants that specialise in Estonian cuisine always offer plenty of other, less daunting, choices for visitors who want to enjoy the traditional ambience without the jellied pork. A casual place to try this food is the **Eesti Maja** restaurant (Lauteri 1, tel: 6455 252) with its eclectic décor. The folksy **Kuldse Notsu Kõrts** (Dunkri, tel: 6286 576) and the 1930s-style **Vanaema Juures** (Rataskaevu 10, tel: 6269 080) are worthwhile choices in the Old Town.

The Modern Menu

While nearly all Estonians will talk of traditional countryside food with patriotic, misty-eyed reverie, the truth is that hardly any of them will have it more than a cou-

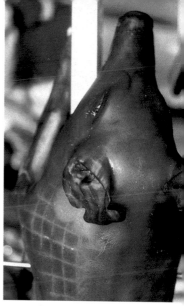

Pork is the favourite meat

ple times a year, if at all. What locals are more likely to eat when they eat out is the simple, cheap and filling fare served in pubs and lunch cafés. Meals here typically consist of a piece of fried meat served with the obligatory side dish of boiled potatoes, a bit of cabbage or carrot, and a couple of slices of fresh tomato and cucumber. For the main item, *sealiha* (pork) is the definite favourite, with pork chops and pork *šnitsel* topping most menus. *Piprapihv* (pepper steak), *kanafilee* (chicken fillet), *grillitud forell* (grilled salmon), lamb and other basic meat dishes are also common.

Russian dishes such as *seljanka*, a meaty soup, and *pelmeenid*, a kind of ravioli served in a broth, are so widespread that many locals think of them as Estonian. Another favourite, particularly in summer, is *šašlõkk*, a shish kebab that comes from the Caucasus region.

A much more recent trend in Estonia is the addition of exotic types of Baltic game to restaurant menus. A few establishments have started to serve elk, deer, bear and wild boar to curious carnivores. One Indian restaurant, **Elevant** (Vene 5, tel: 6313 132), even has a moose curry. Look for other versions of these unusual meats in restaurants around the Old Town.

When Ordering

Though it's mainly straightforward, the Estonian menu has a few nuances that can be confusing to foreigners. For instance, when ordering, it's important to keep in mind that a 'salad' is usually a mixture of finely chopped meat, rice, potatoes or vegetables mixed with mayonnaise and served in a small dish. Anyone looking for a low-calorie plate of let-

Vegetarian Options

The idea of anyone willingly giving up meat is fairly baffling to the pork-chop-loving Estonians, so it's no surprise that Tallinn has no exclusively vegetarian restaurants. But vegetarians won't starve. Catering as they do to the international market, many restaurants in the Old Town have made one or two *taimetoidud* (vegetarian dishes) available. These range from fairly uninspired concoctions of stir-fried veggies or grilled cauliflower to very decent potato pancakes or stews. Note that salads and soups that would seem to be meat-free by their menu descriptions will often contain bits of ham. Consulting the waiter when ordering is the best way to avoid any surprises.

Ethnic restaurants, particularly Indian, Thai and Chinese, usually have the most promising vegetarian selections, often with a whole page of options. Italian restaurants will always have a pasta or pizza dish that is made without meat.

tuce, carrots, olives and the like should order a 'green salad' or consult the waiter for advice. A 'sandwich' in the local understanding is a single, small piece of bread topped with a simple piece of cheese, meat or fish.

Another twist is that pancakes, *pannkoogid*, are not primarily a breakfast food. Thick pancakes with savoury fillings such as ham and cheese, tuna, mushrooms and prawn are often served as a snack or a main lunch course, while honey-

Ordering a bite to eat at the Peppersack restaurant

or jam-filled pancakes make popular desserts. Similarly, omelettes can just as easily be ordered for lunch or dinner as they can for breakfast.

After ordering, a basket of bread usually arrives at your table. The bread is always free, and its freshness is a good indicator of the quality of the food to come. Water, by contrast, does not come free as it does in many other countries, and has to be ordered by the glass or bottle.

Snacks

Jäätis (ice cream) is the undisputed king of summertime snacks. Countless varieties are available from street vendors, shops and kiosks all over town. Other snacks include fresh strawberries, sometimes sold by teenagers milling through the Old Town, and roasted almonds covered in sugar and cinnamon that can be bought from an old-fashioned covered wagon.

Almost as popular (but no more healthy) are the beer snacks served in restaurants and pubs. *Küüslauguleivad*, or garlic bread, which in the Estonian case is made of small, oily pieces of black bread, is the most popular of these. Another one to try, if your arteries can stand it, is *juustupallid*, or fried cheese balls.

Dessert

Estonian restaurants always have plenty of *magustoidud* (desserts) to satisfy the most ravenous sweet tooth. *Pannkoogid* (pancakes) are highly popular and can be found on almost every menu. They come with a fruit, jam or honey filling, and can also be accompanied by the nation's other favourite, *jäätis* (ice cream). A truly unforgettable variation of ice cream that every visitor should try is the one with the city's famous Vana Tallinn liqueur *(see page 89)* dribbled over it.

The Estonians have a well developed sweet tooth

Koogid (cakes) of various sorts are often available. The most typically Estonian (and delicious) of these are the ones made on a base of *kohupiim*, a kind of sweet cream cheese.

The time-honoured Estonian treat is *kama*, a thick mixture of grains and sour milk *(keefir)* that is served in the 'traditional' establishments. The curious will want to give it a try, but many foreigners find it simply too bizarre for their tastes.

Drinks

When it comes to beverages, the nation's clear choice is **beer** *(õlu)*. The unquestionable favourites among the Estonian brews are the two lagers, Saku Originaal and A. Le Coq Premium. One or the other can be found in almost every pub, café or restaurant. When trying other names, you may have to choose between a *hele* (light) or *tume* (dark) beer. Imports of popular international beers are also available, albeit at a higher price.

Coming in a close second to beer in popularity is Estonian **vodka** *(viin)*. The Saaremaa Viin and Viru Valge brands are recommended. **Wine** *(vein)* has also been gaining popularity in recent years, particularly with the emergence of several elegant wine bars in the Old Town *(see page 84)*. Wines from all corners of the globe, from Chile to Moldova, can be found on local menus.

Vana Tallinn, the city's signature liqueur, may look like something very old and traditional judging by its label, but it was invented in the 1960s as a kind of souvenir. Few locals drink the sweet, dark liquid by itself. It works best when added to coffee or used to liven up a dessert.

The Estonian Toast

Estonians aren't ones for long speeches; when they toast, they simply clink their glasses and say '*terviseks!*' ('to your health'). When going through this process though, it is absolutely vital to make eye-to-eye contact with each person as your glasses touch. Failure to do so is considered rude, and can lead to calls for you to repeat the toast the correct way.

Finally, when the weather turns cold, there's no substitute for *hõõgvein*, a hot, spiced wine drink similar to Swedish *glögg*. A cup or two of *hõõgvein* at Christmas is enough to put anyone in the holiday spirit.

To Help You Order...

Could we have a table?	**Palun kas me saaksime laua?**
I'd like a/an/some...	**Ma sooviksin...**
The bill, please.	**Palun arvet.**

bread	**leib**	potatoes	**kartulid**
butter	**või**	rice	**riis**
coffee	**kohv**	salad	**salat**
dessert	**dessert/ magustoit**	salt	**sool**
		sandwich	**võileib**
fish	**kala**	soup	**supp**
fruit	**puuvili**	sugar	**suhkur**
ice cream	**jäätis**	tea	**tee**
meat	**liha**	wine	**vein**
menu	**menüü**	vegetarian	**taimetoitlane**
milk	**piim**	vodka	**viin**
pepper	**pipar**		

...and Read the Menu

eelroad	starters	**kaste**	sauce
forell	trout	**koha**	pike
hapukapsas	sauerkraut	**kohv**	coffee
jäätis	ice cream	**köögiviljad**	vegetables
juust	cheese	**koor**	cream
kala	fish	**krevetid**	prawn
kalkun	turkey	**kurk**	cucumber
kana	chicken	**lasteroad**	children's menu
kartulid	potatoes		

leib	dark bread	**sealiha**	pork
liha	meat	**seened**	mushrooms
lisandid	side orders	**sink**	ham
lõhe	salmon	**supid**	soups
magustoidud	desserts	**suupisted**	appetisers
õlu	beer	**taimeoidud**	vegetarian dishes
omletid	omelettes	**tee**	tea
pannkoogid	pancakes	**tomat**	tomato
pardiliha	duck	**tuunikala**	tuna
piim	milk	**vein**	wine
porgand	carrot	**veiseliha**	beef
praed	main courses	**viin**	vodka
riis	rice	**vesi**	water
sai	white bread		
salatid	salads		

Sült, a jellied meat dish made from pork

HANDY TRAVEL TIPS

An A–Z Summary of Practical Information

A

ACCOMMODATION

Hotels in the centre of Tallinn generally come in two varieties: small, stylish, exclusive establishments within the Old Town, and large, towering, chain-type hotels just outside the Old Town. In both cases the prices can vary substantially even for the same level of quality, so comparison-shopping is always a good idea. Bear in mind that many hotels, including the chains, offer discounts of 5–15 percent to customers booking over the Internet. Bargain hunters should also note that rates for equivalent hotels located a short distance from the centre can be as much as 30–40 percent lower.

For travellers staying three days or more, renting a flat is an alternative worth considering. An increasing number of firms specialise in accommodation rentals, offering smart, fully equipped apartments in the Old Town for the same price as a double room in a hotel. Prices per night become cheaper the longer you stay.

Anyone on a tight budget should first try to find space in one of the few guesthouses and hostels in the Old Town, then look at what's available further out. Family-run guesthouses and a few Soviet-era dormitories that have been turned into hotels provide super-cheap accommodation on Tallinn's periphery. Rooms in private homes in the centre of town can be booked through Rasastra (tel: 6616 291, <www.bedbreakfast.ee>).

In all cases, booking well in advance is essential. During Tallinn's peak season, May to August, beds become scarce. Tallinn has no central booking service. If you arrive without accommodation, you should visit the Tourist Information Centre *(see page 126)*. They will provide you with suggestions and hotel contacts, but you will have to make the calls yourself.

The best resource for accommodation information is the Tallinn Tourism Office's extensive website <www.tourism.tallinn.ee>, where the definitive list of the city's registered hotels, guesthouses, hostels and apartments can be found. The list helpfully includes price categories and links to each hotel's own site.

I've a reservation.	**Mul on tuba broneeritud.**
I'd like a ... room ...	**Ma sooviksin ... tuba ...**
single/double	**ühelist/kahelist**
with a bath/shower	**vanniga/dušiga**

AIRPORT

Completely revamped in 1998, Tallinn Airport is one of Europe's most modern. However, with just six gates, it's also one of Europe's smallest. That means it's extremely easy to find your way around, and you can be out of the door very soon after you exit the plane.

Arrival and departure areas are located in two halves of the same long hall. As you enter the arrival area after clearing customs, ATMs and banks are to your left, towards the centre of the hall. An information desk just beyond them only provides details on the airport itself and how to get into town. Car-hire companies are all downstairs.

Taxis and buses wait just outside the arrivals area's main door, straight ahead. The airport is close to the centre of town, so an airport transfer by taxi can take as little as 10 minutes. The fare should be 70–80kr. City bus No. 2, which will take you to a stop next to the Viru shopping mall in the centre, departs from the airport every 20–30 minutes. Its timetable is posted under the blue-and-white bus sign outside. The 10-minute journey costs 15kr. Pay the driver as you board.

What bus do I take to the centre?	**Missugune buss sôidab kesklinna?**
How much is the fare to ...?	**Kui palju maksab pilet ...?**
Will you tell me when to get off?	**Palun öelge kus ma pean väljuma?**

B

BICYCLE HIRE (RENTAL)

Getting around by bicycle isn't easy in the tourist-packed Old Town, but it's a perfect way to explore the leafy Kadriorg district, the Pirita beach area and the shoreline that stretches between them.

City Bike (tel: 5111 819, <www.citybike.ee>), operating out of the Comfort Hotel Oru in Kadriorg, hires out bikes for periods of one hour (35kr) to one day (225kr). The price includes safety equipment and locks. You must leave a €100 deposit or a document, such as a passport, in the hotel's safe. The firm can deliver and pick up bicycles from other locations. City Bike also hires out bicycles at the Estonian Open Air Museum, and in summer they organise daily bicycle tours of the city.

BUDGETING FOR YOUR TRIP

Airport transfer. By taxi to the centre: 80kr; by city bus: 15kr.

Buses and trams. Tickets cost 10kr from a kiosk, 15kr from the driver, and are valid for one trip. A book of 10 tickets from a kiosk costs 70kr.

Car hire. A compact car costs around 900kr per day if hired from an international rental agency and 600kr from a local company. For a mid-sized car, expect to pay 1,400kr to an international agency and 1,000kr to a local company.

Entertainment. Mid-range tickets to a symphony concert average 250kr, premium cinema tickets cost 110kr, and entrance to a popular nightclub costs 100–50kr on weekends.

Food and drink. A meal, without drinks, typically costs between 110 and 160kr per person. In the most expensive restaurants, it's 500–600kr. A large beer in a local pub costs 25kr, and in a touristy café such as those on Town Hall Square, 40kr. Soft drinks are usually priced at about 15kr.

Hotels. The rate for a double room in a mid-range hotel is 1,500–2,000kr, but quite decent rooms can be found for under 1,000kr.

Museums. Museum tickets for adults cost 10–25kr.

Tallinn Card. Available in 24-, 48- and 72-hour versions at 250, 300 and 350kr respectively, a Tallinn Card gives holders free access to all of the city's museums, free use of public transport and discounts in a number of shops and restaurants. Consider carefully before buying one on a Monday or Tuesday, when many museums are closed. Cards are sold at the Tourist Information Centre *(see page 126)* and at larger hotels.

Travel to Tallinn. In general, return tickets from North America cost US$1,000–$1,400, and from London as low as £50 with the budget airline Easyjet, and from £200 for other carriers. Travelling from Europe by Eurolines coach <www.eurolines. com> is fairly cheap. A single ticket from Berlin is under €90, and from Riga, under €13.

C

CAMPING

The only real campsite near Tallinn is operated by the Hotel Peoleo (Pärnu Mantee 555, Laagri, tel: 6503 965, <www.peoleo.ee>), near a highway 15km (9 miles) from the centre. A fee of 70kr allows you to pitch your tent and entitles you to use the shower and toilets. Strictly speaking, a tent isn't even necessary – like most Estonian 'kämping' sites, this one has simple, little camp huts. All you really need is a sleeping bag and your mosquito repellent. Caravan parking, with electricity and water connection, is available here for 190kr.

CAR HIRE (RENTAL)

Unless you plan to travel around the countryside during your stay, there's no real need to hire a car when visiting Tallinn. Nearly all the important sites are within easy walking distance of one another; the rest can be reached with a short tram or bus ride.

Most of the major international hire-car agencies operate in the city. All have rental desks on the lower floor of Tallinn Airport, and some also have offices in the city centre.

The daily rental price of a mid-sized car, such as a Ford Mondeo, is around 1,500kr. Local agencies, like Sir Autorent and R-Rent listed below, will charge about 900kr for the same model. Automatic cars are a rarity, and should be requested in advance. Mileage is unlimited, but hirers are expected to fill the tank just before returning the car. To hire a car, a driver must be at least 21 years of age, possess a valid driving licence with photo, and must have held a licence for at least two years.

Avis: at the airport, tel: 6058 222; in the city at Liivalaia 13/15, tel: 6671 500, <www.avis.ee>.
Budget: at the airport, tel: 6058 600, <www.budget.ee>.
Hertz: at the airport, tel. 6058 923; in the city at Ahtri 12, tel: 6116 333, <www.hertz.ee>.
R-Rent: at the airport, tel: 6612 400, <www.rrent.ee>.
Sir Rent: Juhkentali 11, tel: 6614 353, <www.sirrent.ee>.
Sixt: at the airport, tel: 6058 148; in the city at Rävala 5, tel: 6133 660, <www.sixt.ee>.

I'd like to hire a car.	**Ma sooviksin üürida autot.**
I'd like it for a day/week.	**Ma sooviksin seda üheks päevaks nädalaks.**
Where's the nearest petrol station?	**Kus on lähim bensiinijaam?**

CLIMATE

Winter days can be either bitterly cold or uncomfortably damp. Spring and autumn are unpredictable, with temperatures hovering just above freezing. The best time to visit is unquestionably summer when the weather is mildest and the northern skies stay light until after 11pm, although June and July are also the wettest months, and can bring heavy rain showers. The following chart shows the average monthly highs and lows in Tallinn:

	J	F	M	A	M	J	J	A	S	O	N	D
°C	0	-1	2	9	13	19	22	20	15	10	3	0
	-5	-7	-5	0	3	9	11	10	6	3	-1	-5
°F	32	29	36	49	56	66	71	69	60	50	38	31
	22	17	22	32	38	48	53	51	43	38	29	22

CLOTHING

Sensible, casual clothing will suit most occasions. Light, summer attire is perfect for touring the city in the high season, but keep in mind that warm, sunny days can quickly turn cool, so it's always a good idea to carry along an extra layer of clothing. A light, waterproof jacket will also come in handy as sudden rain showers are not uncommon. Anyone visiting Tallinn in winter should pack heavy coats, scarves, gloves, boots – and a sense of humour. For touring the uneven, cobbled streets of the Old Town, sturdy shoes are a must.

Smart dress is the norm for diners in moderate to expensive restaurants. The same is true of nightclubs.

CRIME AND SAFETY

Your chances of becoming the victim of a crime are remote, but the city is not crime-free. The most common offences against foreigners involve petty theft, an activity that's concentrated in the Old Town, on Viru Street in particular. Take care that your wallet isn't temptingly jutting from your pocket, and that your bag, camera or mobile phone isn't sitting too close to the outer rail of the café. Leave valuables in your hotel, preferably in the safe, and keep your car in a guarded car park at night, as vehicle break-ins are also a problem in Tallinn.

Violent crime against foreigners is rare, but you can use common sense to reduce the risk. Avoid unfamiliar, unlit areas at night, particularly if you're alone. Drink responsibly, and don't end up stumbling out of a pub late at night with a group of strangers.

Call the police.	**Kutsuge politsei.**
My ... has been stolen.	**Minu ... on ära varastatud.**
handbag/wallet	**käekoti/rahakoti**
Stop thief!	**Peatage varas!**
Help!	**Appi!**
Leave me alone!	**Jätke mind rahule!**

CUSTOMS AND ENTRY REQUIREMENTS

Passports/Visas. Citizens of the European Union, US, Canada, Australia, New Zealand, and at least 30 other countries can enter Estonia and stay for up to 90 days without a visa. The complete list of countries whose citizens can enter without a visa can be found on the Estonian Foreign Ministry's website, <www.vm.ee>. Citizens of all other countries require visas, which they can obtain at their nearest Estonian consulate. South Africans don't need an Estonian visa if they hold a valid visa for Latvia or Lithuania.

EU and EEA citizens can enter Estonia using a national ID card in lieu of a passport. Everyone else entering Estonia must have a valid passport.

Vaccinations. You do not need any special vaccinations to visit Estonia, unless you plan to explore a forested area *(see page 117)*.

Currency Restrictions. There are no restrictions on how much currency you can import or export, but you're required to declare any amount exceeding €15,000.

Customs. When arriving from outside the EU, you can import the following goods duty free: 2 litres of wine, 1 litre of spirits, 2 litres of other (non-spirit) alcoholic beverages and up to €175 worth of beer; 200 cigarettes, or 100 cigarillos, or 50 cigars, or 250g of smoking tobacco or 250g of chewing tobacco.

By contrast, when arriving from another EU country, you can import the following goods duty free: 90 litres of wine, 110 litres of beer, 10 litres of spirits and 20 litres of other (non-spirit) alcoholic beverages; 800 cigarettes, 400 cigarillos, 200 cigars, 1kg of smoking tobacco and 1kg of chewing tobacco. When travelling from Estonia to another EU country, the same levels usually apply, but there are sometimes special restrictions. For example, you can only take 200 cigarettes from Estonia to Finland.

Exporting antiques. Note that antiques bought in Estonia cannot be exported without a permit. This applies to anything made in Estonia before 1945 and anything made elsewhere before 1850. Antique dealers are familiar with these rules and should be able to assist you with the paperwork.

D

DRIVING

Road conditions. Road conditions in Estonia are generally good, both in Tallinn and on motorways. The biggest hazard is usually other drivers, whose habits range from the careless to the aggressive. Your only recourse is to drive defensively. Weather is the next issue, particularly in winter when patches of ice appear on streets and roads. If you don't know how to drive in winter conditions, this is not the place to learn. Also, because markings on rural routes can often be confusing, a good road atlas is essential. Finally, drivers unfamiliar with Tallinn should avoid the Old Town, with its confusing system of one-way streets.

Road signs. Traffic signs and symbols in Estonia follow the European standard.

Rules and regulations. Drive on the right and overtake on the left. Estonian law requires that headlights be kept on at all times, day and night, even in the city. The basic speed limit outside built-up areas is 90km/h (56mph), in built-up areas 50km/h (31mph), and in residential areas 20km/h (13mph). Some roads are marked with their own limits, particularly large motorways, where cars are permitted to travel at 110km/h (69mph) in summer. In the city, passengers in both front seats must wear seatbelts at all times. On motorways, the same rule applies to back-seat passengers as well. Children under 12 are not allowed in the front seat. Winter tyres must be used from 15 October to 15 April, though the dates can change from year to year. Valid foreign driving licences can be used in Estonia for up to a year; no international licence is needed.

Filling up. First pump, then pay. Fuel comes in four varieties: 92, 95, 98 and diesel. Most drivers use the 95 or higher quality 98. A litre of fuel generally costs 10–11kr.

Parking. Finding somewhere to park in Tallinn's busy centre can be a true test of will. Most street parking is paid parking. Tickets are sold in vending machines and cost either 3 or 6kr per 15 minutes. They should be displayed on the dashboard along with a marking clock (usually provided by car-hire companies) or a note indicating the time you parked. Car parks/garages can be found in central Tallinn on Freedom Square (Vabaduse väljak), on Rävala 5, and at the corner of Maakri and Rävala. The cost is typically 20kr per hour

If you need help. Dial 118 for road service. They will tow your car to the nearest garage. If you need an ambulance, dial 112; police, 110.

Are we on the right road for ...?	**Kas me oleme õigel teel ...?**
Fill the tank, please with ...	**Palun täitke paak**
92/95/98/diesel	**92/95/98/diisel**
My car's broken down.	**Mu auto läks katki.**
There's been an accident.	**Juhtus õnnetus.**

E

ELECTRICITY

The electricity in Estonia is 220 volts AC, 50Hz. Plugs are the round, two-pinned variety used in continental Europe, and adaptors can be found in electronic shops and in department stores.

EMBASSIES AND CONSULATES

Note that some embassies that serve Estonia are not in Estonia.

Australia. Sergels Torg 12, Stockholm, Sweden; tel: (+46 8) 613 29 00.
Canada. (Representative office only) Toomkooli 13, Tallinn; tel: 6273 311.
Ireland. Vene 2, Tallinn; tel: 6811 888.
South Africa. Rahapajankatu 1 A 5, Helsinki, Finland; tel: (+358 9) 686 03 100.
UK. Wismari 6, Tallinn; tel: 6674 700.
US. Kentmanni 20, Tallinn; tel: 6688 100.

Where is the British/American Embassy?	**Kus on Inglise/Ameerika saatkond?**

EMERGENCIES

Police 110
Fire 112
Paramedics 112

| Where can I find a doctor who speaks English? | **Kust ma vôiksin leida arsti, kes räägib inglise keelt?** |

G

GAY AND LESBIAN TRAVELLERS

Though the situation is improving, attitudes towards homosexuality in Estonia have not caught up to those in the West. Overt displays, such as holding hands, may attract the wrong sort of attention. Tallinn has a small but active gay night scene encompassing a handful of bars and clubs. X-Baar (Sauna 1) is the most central of these, but G-Punkt (Pärnu Mantee 23) is more popular.

GETTING TO TALLINN

From the UK

The budget airline Easyjet (<www.easyjet.com>) – flying from Stansted – and the nation's flag-carrier Estonian Air (tel: 020 7333 0196, <www.estonianair.ee>) – flying from Gatwick – operate direct flights between London and Tallinn. Other airlines, such as SAS (<www.scandinavian.net>) and Finnair (tel: 0870/241 4411, <www.finnair.com>), offer flights that connect through Copenhagen and Helsinki respectively, though these routes are usually more expensive.

UK-based agencies Baltic Holidays (tel: 0870/757 9233, <www.balticholidays.com>) and Regent Holidays (tel: 0117/921 1711, <www.regent-holidays.co.uk>) specialise in travel to the Baltics and can offer good deals.

From outside Europe

There are two basic strategies: get the best deal you can on a flight to London, then take an Easyjet or Estonian Air flight *(see above)*, or use one of the airlines that can connect you to Tallinn through its regional hub. The major airlines with services to Tallinn are Finnair, SAS, Lufthansa, CSA Czech Airlines and LOT Polish Airways. If all else fails, you can try to find a cheap flight to Helsinki and take a ferry south to Tallinn.

From neighbouring countries

If you're travelling from elsewhere in the Baltics or Central Europe, the bus, not the train, is the way to go. Eurolines (<www.eurolines.com>) offer frequent connections and good rates. From Northern Europe, overnight ferries make a slow but inexpensive connection from Stockholm, and each day dozens of ships make the quick, 85-km (53-mile) crossing from Helsinki.

GUIDES AND TOURS

Tourism in Tallinn is heavily orientated towards groups, who tend to arrange their own excursions, but the city does offer a couple of tours that individuals can join. The most popular is the Tallinn Official Sightseeing Tour operated by Reisiekspert (tel: 6108 634), a combination bus and walking tour that covers all the city's major sights. It runs three times daily and costs 200kr (free with Tallinn Card, *see page 108*). You can also opt to meet the group for the walking tour only; this costs 100kr. Phone for timetables and meeting places. A more adventurous option is the Welcome to Tallinn bicycle tour organised by City Bike (tel: 5111 819). It departs every evening at 5pm, operating May to September. The tour covers the city's outlying green districts, the beach area and the Old Town. The 30kr tour price includes bicycle rental and mineral water, and pick-up is available from three major hotels. Prior booking is required.

You can also book your own, private guide through Tourist Information *(see page 126)*. Guides cost 350kr per hour, irrespective of the size of the group, and have to be hired for a minimum of 1½ hours. Book at least 48 hours in advance.

Is there an English-speaking guide?	**Kas teil on inglise keelt kônelev giid?**
Can you translate this for me?	**Kas te oskate seda mulle tôlkida?**

H

HEALTH AND MEDICAL CARE

Visiting Estonia poses no significant health risks. The water is perfectly safe and, thanks to Scandinavian technology, tastes much better than it has in years. One concern however, which only applies to visitors who spend time deep in the Estonian wilderness, is tick-borne encephalitis. If you plan to explore a forested area, you should get a vaccination before leaving home.

Western-produced medicines, including many of the same brands you would find at home, are widely available from any pharmacy *(apteek)*. Staff in central locations generally speak English. In this small country, selection is limited, so if you need a very specialised product, it's best to bring it with you. The Tõnismäe Apteek (Tõnismägi 5, tel: 6442 282) runs an all-night pharmacy window.

The state-run hospitals in Estonia are hit-and-miss in terms of service, and most foreigners use them only if absolutely necessary. The standards at private clinics are much better, but these generally don't provide emergency services. If you have a medical problem, you can contact Tallinn's Central Hospital (*Keskhaigla*; Ravi 18, tel: 6027 015). Tallinn's paramedic service also runs a first-aid hotline (tel: 6971 145) that can give you advice or direct you to a hospital. If an ambulance is needed, call 112.

Where's the nearest (all night) pharmacy?	**Kus on lähim (ööpäev lahti olev) apteek?**
I need a doctor/dentist. an ambulance	**Ma vajan arsti/hambaarsti kiirabi**
hospital	**haigla**
an upset stomach	**kõht on korrast ära**
I have a stomach ache/ sunburn/a fever.	**Minu kõht valutab/ päikesepõletus/palavik.**

HOLIDAYS

The following are public holidays in Estonia when banks, shops and offices are closed. Restaurants, cafés and bars usually close only on Christmas, New Year's Day and Midsummer.

New Year's Day	1 January
Independence Day (1918)	24 February
Good Friday and Easter	March or April
Spring Day	1 May
Victory Day	23 June
Midsummer Day (St John's Day)	24 June
Day of Restoration of Independence	20 August
Christmas	25 December
Boxing Day	26 December

LANGUAGE

The national language is Estonian, a Finno-Ugric tongue related to Finnish and Hungarian, but completely unrecognisable to Estonia's other neighbours. Its complicated grammatical structure and baffling vowels have given it the reputation of being one of the world's most difficult languages to learn. Fortunately, English is widely spoken in the capital, and you should have no trouble communicating.

Stress is almost always on the first syllable. Double vowels are pronounced exactly the same as single vowels, only twice as long. The same applies to double consonants. 'J' is pronounced as a 'y.'

Pronunciation of vowels
a as in 'palm'
ä as in 'cat'
e as in 'set'
i as in 'me'
o as in 'cold'
ö as in the German 'öl' or the French 'deux'
õ has no equivalent. Smile and say 'oh'
u as in 'moon'
ü as in the German 'für' or the French 'sur'

Do you speak English?	**Kas te räägite inglise keelt?**
Hello	**Tere**
Goodbye	**Head aega/nägemist**
Pardon me	**Vabandust**
Please	**Palun**
Thank you	**Aitäh**
Cheers!	**Terviseks!**

M

MAPS

Free maps are available at the Tourist Information Centre *(see page 126)*. Additionally, all the free tourist/shopping guides floating around Tallinn will have a map of the Old Town you can tear out. More detailed maps, such as the one published by Jana Seta, can be found in the Apollo bookshop, Viru 23.

MEDIA

Television Most hotels have cable or satellite hook-ups that bring in the international news channels. Estonia itself only has three broadcasters, but much of the entertainment programming is in English with Estonian subtitles.

Radio The BBC World Service is broadcast daily 9am–11am and 3pm–5.30pm on Estonian Radio, 103.5MHz FM. Estonian Radio also broadcast a daily news bulletin in English Mon–Fri at 6pm.

Press International newspapers are sold in major hotels and in the larger R-Kiosks in central Tallinn. They also sell *The Baltic Times*, an English-language weekly that covers regional news and culture. A handful of English-language city guides can be found in town, but the best of the bunch is the invaluable *Tallinn In Your Pocket*, a slightly cheeky, bi-monthly publication that features everything from restaurant and nightclub listings to museum prices.

MONEY

The currency is the crown or the *kroon*, abbreviated kr or EEK. Its value is fixed at 15.646kr to the euro. One *kroon* is made of 100 *senti*. Bank notes come in denominations of 500kr, 100kr, 50kr, 25kr, 10kr, 5kr and 2kr, and there are 1kr, 50 *senti*, 20 *senti* and 10 *senti* coins.

Currency Exchange

Exchanging money in Tallinn is quick and easy during regular business hours. There are several banks and exchange offices operating in the Old Town and the centre. No documents are required and there's no hidden commission; the rate you see posted is the rate you'll get. Most exchanges are closed on weekends and in the evenings. Monex operates brightly painted exchanges that stay open late and on weekends, including one right on Town Hall Square, but rates here are significantly worse than elsewhere. Tavid (Aia 5) operates a 24-hour exchange window that will do in a necessity.

Credit Cards

All but the smallest restaurants, shops and hotels accept Visa, Visa Electron, MasterCard and Maestro. American Express can be used in the larger hotels, but is not widely accepted by local businesses.

ATMs

ATMs are easy to find in central Tallinn, and nearly all will allow you to withdraw money using your bank card or credit card. Check with your own bank before leaving home.

Travellers' Cheques

Travellers' cheques from major issuers such as Thomas Cook and American Express are exchangeable at most banks, but are not accepted as payment in shops, restaurants or hotels.

Can I pay with this credit card?	**Kas ma saan selle krediitkaardiga maksta?**
I want to change some pounds/dollars	**Ma soovin vahetada naelasid/dollareid.**
Can you cash a travellers' cheque?	**Kas te saaksite reisitšekke rahaks vahetada?**
Where's the nearest bank/ currency exchange office?	**Kus on lähim pank/valuutavahetus?**
Is there a cash machine near here?	**Kas lähedal on pangaautomaat?**
How much is that?	**Kui palju see maksab?**

O

OPENING HOURS

Opening hours vary from business to business, but most follow these general customs:

Bank are open 9am–5 or 6pm Monday to Friday, with some of the larger branches open 10am–3pm on Saturday. Business offices and government offices work 9am–5pm Monday to Friday.

Museums are open 11am–6pm. Most are closed Monday and/or Tuesday.

Small shops and fashion boutiques open at 10am and close 5–7pm Monday to Friday. Some are closed Saturdays, but most open 10am–3 or 4pm. Small shops are almost always closed Sundays. Department stores and shopping centres, on the other hand, stay open much later. These are open 9am–9pm daily, sometimes closing an hour or two earlier on Sundays.

Restaurants, unless they also operate as pubs or nightclubs, generally open at 11am or noon and close at 11pm or midnight. Some stay open one or two hours later on Friday and Saturday nights. Sundays are slow for restaurants, prompting a few to close their doors at 6pm. On weekends, the popular bars and pubs in the Old Town stay open until 3 or 4am.

P

POLICE

Estonia's police can be seen roving the streets in pairs, wearing dark blue jumpsuits with the word 'Politsei' emblazoned across the back. Those assigned to the Old Town usually understand at least some English or will call a colleague who can. If you find yourself in need of the police, you can call 110 from any phone. You can also report a crime in person at the police station at Pärnu mantee 11, adjacent to the Old Town.

Where's the nearest police station?	**Kus on lähim politseijaoskond?**
I've lost my wallet/ bag/passport	**Kaotasin oma rahakoti/ koti/passi.**

POST OFFICE

For any postal services, Tallinn's Central Post Office (*Peapostkontor*), located at Narva mnt. 1 across from the Viru Hotel, should be your first stop. It's open 7.30am–8pm Monday to Friday, 8am–6pm Saturday, and English-speakers are plentiful. Letters and faxes are sent from the main hall upstairs, and packages from a ground-floor office on the left side of the building.

Stamps are also sold in most kiosks. Tariffs for international mail are as follows: to the Baltics and Scandinavia: postcards 5kr, letters 6kr; elsewhere in Europe, including UK and Ireland: postcards 6kr, letters 6.50kr; everywhere else: postcards 7.50kr, letters 8kr. Drop your postcards and letters in any of the small, orange post boxes you see around town.

Where's the nearest post office?	**Kus on lähim postkontor?**
express (special delivery)	**kullerteenus registered**

PUBLIC TRANSPORT

Mass transit. A system of buses, trams and electric trolleybuses makes up Tallinn's public transport system. The trams mainly service the centre of town, whereas the buses and trolleybuses are for reaching outlying areas. Detailed maps posted on most bus stops will show you how to make your journey. All three modes of transport use the same ticket, which is available from a kiosk for 10kr (a book of 10 is 70kr), or from the driver for 15kr. When you board, you don't need to show the ticket to the driver, but you must punch it after you board (officials periodically conduct spot checks to make sure tickets have been punched). Each ticket is good for one ride.

Holders of the Tallinn Card, which is available from the Tourist Information Office *(see page 126)* and larger hotels, are entitled to unlimited free use of public transport, in addition to reduced entry prices for many of the city's major museums and attractions *(see page 108)*.

Taxis. The biggest complaint among tourists is taxi drivers who overcharge. This is so common that even locals have the same difficulty. The best strategy is to order a taxi by phone. Controllers at Linnatakso, tel: 1242, and Tulika Takso, tel: 1200 usually speak some English.

Standard rates for taxis are as follows: 10–25kr starting fee (avoided when ordering by phone), then 7kr/km. If in doubt, ask a driver for an estimate before getting in the car.

Where can I get a taxi?	**Kust ma saaksin takso?**
What's the fare to … (the centre)?	**Palju maksab … (keslinna)?**
Take me to this address.	**Viige mind sel aadressil.**
Where is the nearest bus stop?	**Kus on lähim bussipeatus?**
When's the next bus to ...?	**Millal läheb järmine buss …?**
I want a ticket to ... single/return	**Palun üks pilet….sse. üks suund/edasitagasi**
How much is a ticket to … (Tartu)?	**Palju maksab pilet … (Tartusse)?**
Will you tell me when to get off?	**Kas te ütlete millal, ma pean maha minema?**

R

RELIGION

Most people in Estonia are nominally Lutheran, though there is no official state religion and most Estonians are not regular church-goers. Russian Orthodoxy is almost as common as Lutheranism, particularly among Estonia's sizeable ethnic Russian community. Beautiful, medieval churches in Tallinn's Old Town conduct services in an unforgettable atmosphere. The Holy Spirit Church, Pühavaimu 2, holds Anglican services in English each Sunday at 3pm. Tallinn's synagogue is located at Karu 16, tel: 6623 050.

T

TELEPHONE

The Estonian telephone system is on a par with the world's best. Fixed line numbers in Tallinn have seven digits and all begin with a '6'. Mobile numbers begin with a '5'.

To phone Estonia from abroad, dial your international access code (00), Estonia's country code (372), and then the number. There are no city codes.

When phoning overseas from Estonia, dial 00, then your country code: US 1; Canada 1; United Kingdom 44; Ireland 353; Australia 61. If you need information or assistance from an operator, or you want to connect to an operator in your own country, dial 16115. Direct access numbers to organisations like AT&T will allow you to make credit-card calls or, in some cases, to reverse the charges (call collect). AT&T: 80 012 001; MCI 80 012 122; Canadian Teleglobe 80 012 011; BT 80 010 441 or 442.

Public telephones in Tallinn use phone cards, available in any newspaper kiosk for 30, 50 or 100kr. Theoretically, you could make an international call from a public phone, but it would involve tricky card changes.

TIME ZONES

Estonia is in the Eastern European Time Zone. Daylight Saving Time is in effect from the last Sunday in March to the last Sunday in October. The following chart shows the time in various cities in summer.

San Francisco	New York	London	**Tallinn**	Sydney
2am	5am	10am	**noon**	7pm

TIPPING

Tipping is a new phenomenon in Estonia and the practice is still somewhat haphazard. Some people tip, some don't. In restaurants you can reward good service with a 10 percent tip. Tips won't be expected for meals in simpler cafés, pubs, or anywhere you pay at the till. Taxi drivers don't get tips, but you can round up to the next 5kr. Hotel porters should get around 20kr, and tour guides for large groups are usually tipped 15–50kr by each person.

TOILETS

In Estonia the WC *(veetsee)* is sometimes marked using a baffling system of triangles. A triangle pointing downward is the men's room (think of a man with large shoulders), and one pointing up is the women's (think of a dress). Otherwise men's and women's are marked Meeste (M) and Naiste (N) respectively. Public toilets usually cost 2–4kr. A free facility complete with disabled access is located on Town Hall Square adjacent to the Troika restaurant.

Where are the toilets?	**Kus on WC (veetsee)?**

TOURIST INFORMATION

Although limited information can be gleaned from a variety of unofficial sources at the airport and at bus and railway stations, the best place to find in-depth, authoritative information is the Tallinn Tourist Information Centre, located in the heart of the Old Town at Niguliste 2/Kullassepa 4, tel: 645 77 77, fax: 645 77 78, <www. tourism.tallinn.ee>.

WEBSITES AND INTERNET CAFÉS

<www.tourism.tallinn.ee> The city's official tourism website is an excellent resource for travel planning.

<www.inyourpocket.com> *Tallinn In Your Pocket*'s extensive site is also an excellent resource.

<www.vm.ee> The Foreign Ministry's site supplies interesting, detailed information on Estonia as a whole.

<www.baltictimes.com> The Baltic Times is the best news source.

WiFi hotspots fill the Old Town, but if you don't have your own laptop, you can visit Kohvik@Grill on Aia 3 (tel: 6271 229), Neo on Väike-Karja 12 (tel: 6282 333) or Demini Kohvik on Viru 1.

Y

YOUTH HOSTELS

What most people think of as youth hostels – lively places with dormitories, helpful facilities and a social atmosphere – are almost non-existent in Tallinn. The one exception is the Vana Tom (Väike-Karja 1, tel: 6313 253, <www.hostel.ee>). A few tiny, private hostels like Alur (Rannamüe 3, tel: 631 1531, <www.alur.ee>) and Old House (Uus 26, tel: 6411 171, <www.oldhouse.ee>) dot the centre.

The larger establishments are at the edge of town, but reachable by bus. These are mainly converted student dormitories made up of double and triple rooms. Academic Hostel (Akadeemia tee 11, tel: 6202 275, <www.academichostel.com>) is by far the nicest of these, while Mahtra (Mahtra 44, tel: 6218 828, <www.mahtra.ee>) is much shabbier. Estonian YHA (Narva mantee 16–25, tel: 6461 455) can give you further options.

Recommended Hotels

Tallinn's world-class business and tourist hotels have lately been joined in the central-city skyline by a number of high-rise hotel buildings, apparently created with a 'bigger is better' philosophy in mind. Meanwhile, several Old Town buildings have been refashioned into intimate, luxury hotels.

The current building trend is almost solely focused on the middle to high end of the market, and what scant few budget hotels there are in the city centre fill up fast. Decent budget options are still available for anyone willing to brave a 10- or 15-minute taxi ride from the centre. There are also a number of tiny, out-of-the-way guesthouses; most are built onto private, suburban homes. Find them listed on the city's official tourism website, <www.tourism.tallinn.ee>.

Despite all the building, Tallinn still suffers from an acute lack of accommodation space in summer. Prior booking is absolutely essential for anyone planning to visit at that time of year.

The symbols below have been used to indicate high-season rates, based on double occupancy with breakfast, VAT included. Hotels listed here have private showers/baths and accept major credit cards unless otherwise indicated.

€€€€€	Over 3000kr
€€€€	2,550–3,000kr
€€€	2,000–2,550kr
€€	1,200–2,000kr
€	Below 1,200kr

OLD TOWN

Barons €€€ *Suur-Karja 7/Väike-Karja 2, tel: 6999 700, fax: 6999 710, <www.baronshotel.ee>.* Steeped in elegance, this small, luxury hotel is housed in a 1912-era former bank building (and it has the original vaults to prove it). Other interior details, including the charming wood-panelled lift, lobby bar, antique furniture and high ceilings, do a wonderful job of re-creating the subdued primness of the early 20th century. Room amenities include Internet connection, mini-bar, hairdryer, bathrobe and slippers.

Domina City €€€ *Vana-Posti 11, tel: 6813 900, fax: 6813 901, <www.dominahotels.ee>.* One look at the marble columns and grand chandeliers in the lobby is enough to show that the Italian owners took extra pains to make this a chic establishment. All 68 rooms are decorated in a smart, vaguely old-fashioned way, but each comes with its own computer and high-speed Internet connection, as well as mini-bar, safe and hairdryer. Suites come complete with kitchenettes.

Imperial €€€ *Nunne 14, tel: 6274 800, fax: 6274 801, <www.imperial.ee>.* Part of the city's medieval wall runs right through this 19th-century building, but the Imperial creates most of its historic ambience with exposed brick and antique photos in its common areas. The hotel's pride and joy is definitely its magnificent, old-fashioned pub, but the sauna hall is also fairly impressive. Rooms are brightly decorated and have Internet connections and hairdryers, as well as all the other standard features. Laundry service is available. 32 rooms.

Meriton Old Town Hotel € *Lai 49, tel: 6141 300, fax: 6141 311, <www.meriton.ee>.* Priced well below its Old Town neighbours, the Meriton is clearly targeting tourists interested in location and affordability above all else. Its 41 rooms are built into a 19th-century office building, and most of them are fairly cramped. This is by no means a no-frills establishment, however. Décor is cheerful, the modern lobby cleverly incorporates part of the old city wall and a medieval-era horse mill, and the bakery/café here is one of the most respected in town.

OldHouse Guesthouse/OldHouse Hostel € *Uus 22/Uus 26, tel: 6411 464, fax: 6411 604, <www.oldhouse.ee>.* Don't read too much into the 'guesthouse' and 'hostel' labels here – amenities and prices in these twin establishments are nearly identical. Each offers simple, modern single and double rooms, as well as larger 'dorm-style' rooms, all with shared bathrooms. The only discernable difference between the two is that the 'hostel' is a touch nicer and has two more of the large rooms. Price includes breakfast and use of guest kitchen. 6 rooms (guesthouse), 12 rooms (hostel).

Old Town Maestro's €€ *Suur-Karja 10, tel: 6262 000, fax: 6313 333, <www.maestrohotel.ee>.* Apart from the ideal location, the most interesting perk in this intimate hotel is the jacuzzi and sauna room on the top floor. Rooms are spacious but otherwise fairly standard. Subtle touches of the 1930s find their way into the décor in the Maestro's common areas, and the entire third floor is reserved for non-smokers. 23 rooms.

Olevi Residents €€ *Olevimägi 4, tel: 6277 650, fax: 6277 651, <www.olevi.ee>.* The charmingly narrow, 14th-century building alone is enough to create a timeless atmosphere, but the little Olevi hotel is also overflowing with antique-style furnishings and décor. The establishment also features a small French/Italian restaurant and in-room Internet access. Ten percent discount with online booking. 37 rooms.

Schlössle €€€€€ *Pühavaimu 13/15, tel: 6997 700, fax: 6997 777, <www.schlossle-hotels.com>.* An elder figure in Tallinn's pantheon of small, luxury hotels, the Schlössle earns its five-star rating with a combination of impressive ambience and impeccable service. Ancient stone and heavy wooden beams give the lobby its medieval look, while rooms are furnished in a lavish, antique style – right down to the polished brass taps. The long list of amenities includes bathrobes, complimentary daily newspapers and a babysitting service. 23 rooms.

St Petersbourg €€€€€ *Rataskaevu 7, tel: 6286 500, fax: 6286 565, <www.schlossle-hotels.com>.* Run by the same group that manages the respected Schlössle *(above)*, this hotel spoils its guests with similar, old-fashioned comforts, as well as an upmarket Russian restaurant and a simpler Estonian restaurant. Operating since the late 19th century, the St Petersbourg is Tallinn's oldest hotel, and decorators have done a good job of re-creating the aristocratic sophistication of that era. Rooms are art deco in style. Be warned that standard rooms are tiny. 27 rooms.

Taanilinna €€ *Uus 6, tel: 6406 700, fax: 6464 306, <www. taanilinna.ee>*. Small and somewhat hidden, the two-storey Taanilinna is much more low-key than its better-known Old Town rivals. Dark, wooden floors, bricks and old-fashioned furnishings in the rooms create an eclectically historic ambience. Rooms are tasteful and fully outfitted, and guests can take advantage of the sauna and cellar wine bar. 20 rooms.

The Three Sisters €€€€ *Pikk 71/Tolli 2, tel: 6306 300, fax: 6306 301, <www.threesistershotel.com>*. Built inside Tallinn's famous Three Sisters, a trio of 14th–15th-century houses, this five-star hotel offers unmatched lavishness from the real candles used in the lobby chandelier to the amazing in-room décor. In addition to the standard amenities, each of the 23 rooms comes with luxury furniture, CD and DVD player, bathrobe and an umbrella. Some rooms have king-sized poster beds and one suite even has its own piano.

Vana Wiru €€ *Viru 11, tel: 6691 500, fax: 6691 501, <www. vanawiru.ee>*. This modern hotel on the Old Town's main shopping street has an enviable location. It also offers an impressive lobby, two saunas, meeting rooms and a comfortable pub. Rooms are tasteful, but otherwise fairly standard, with all the features one would expect from a three-star establishment. Find the entrance around the back, accessible via Müürivahe street. 82 rooms.

TOWN CENTRE

Best Western Hotell Tallink €€€ *Laikmaa 5, tel: 6300 800, fax: 6300 810, <bwhotel.tallink.com>*. This eight-storey, mirrored building looms behind the Viru Centre shopping complex, which is just metres from the Old Town. In addition to its 350 smartly decorated rooms, the hotel offers plenty of other four-star features such as conference facilities, saunas, gift shop, travel agency and, catering to Finnish guests in particular, a karaoke club.

Meriton Grand Hotel Tallinn €€€€ *Toompuiestee 27, tel: 6677 000, fax: 6677 555, <www.meriton.ee>*. Sitting on the opposite edge of the Old Town from Tallinn's main commercial centre, the Grand isn't in the middle of the action. Still, it's within easy walking distance of the town's main sights and has some excellent views of nearby Toompea Castle. It's also considered one of Tallinn's finest hotels, with a top-notch restaurant, a busy café, and a host of services, ranging from conference facilities to dental treatment. 164 rooms.

Radisson SAS €€€ *Rävala pst. 3, tel: 6823 000, fax: 6823 001, <www.radissonsas.com>*. Tallinn's Radisson, a five-minute walk from the Old Town, delivers everything one would expect from a world-class chain hotel. The towering building is the tallest in the city, so ask for a room on the town side for the most interesting views. Its rooms are decorated in Oriental, Italian, Maritime or Scandinavian themes. A large number of conference rooms is available, as are business services, a health club and a cigar shop. The hotel also operates two restaurants and, in summer, a rooftop café. 280 rooms.

Reval Hotel Olümpia €€€ *Liivalaia 33, tel: 6315 333, fax: 6315 325, <www.revalhotels.com>*. This four-star monolith is contemporary looking inside and out despite the fact that it was built for the 1980 Olympic Games. With 390 rooms and an attached conference centre, it's one of the largest hotels in Tallinn, drawing large groups. The hotel also has business facilities, a comfortable restaurant, lunch café, English-style pub and nightclub. In the health club on the 26th floor guests can use a sauna and swimming pool while taking in spectacular views of the city. 10–15 minutes walk from the Old Town.

Scandic Palace €€€€ *Vabaduse väljak 3, tel: 6407 300, fax: 6407 299, <www.scandic-hotels.com>*. A strong dose of 1930s-style class has worked its way into every corner of this historic building, which stands just outside the Old Town and overlooks Freedom Square. It's starting to seem a bit scruffy compared to recent, super-modern four-star arrivals, but few can beat its authentic feel, location or welcoming lobby bar. It also has a sauna, conference facilities and, in some rooms, air conditioning. 86 rooms.

Skåne € *Kopli 2c, tel: 6678 300, fax: 6678 301, <www.nordichotels. ee>.* Skåne opened as a hotel in the early 20th century, and although it has been completely renovated, it retains the feel of that era. Rooms have hardwood floors, modern furniture and come fully equipped. The area behind the railway station where this little hotel is located isn't the best, but the price, quality and the proximity to the Old Town are pluses.

Sokos Viru Hotel €€€ *Viru väljak 4, tel: 6809 300, fax: 6809 236, <www.viru.ee>.* Tallinn's most famous Soviet-era high-rise hotel has evolved into a quality, international establishment that's especially popular with Finnish tour groups. Apart from its enviable location beside the Old Town, the gigantic, Finnish-run hotel offers colourfully decorated rooms, a conference centre, saunas, a beauty salon, countless bars, an upmarket restaurant, a casual Tex-Mex restaurant, and a nightclub. The Viru is also conveniently attached to downtown's largest shopping and dining complex, the Viru Centre. 516 rooms.

Uniquestay €€ *Paldiski mnt. 1, tel: 6600 700, fax: 6616 176, <www.uniquestay.com>.* This modern, British-owned hotel is divided between two brick buildings on the quiet edge of the Old Town, not far from Toompea Castle. The concept here is to offer guests something 'unique', specifically rooms with tasteful, chic designs and Internet-connected computers. For an extra fee, guests can opt for one of the the Zen rooms, which have such extras as NASA-designed, gravity-free chairs, aromatherapy amenities and adjustable lighting. The hotel also has two good cafés. 75 rooms.

PORT AREA

City Hotel Portus € *Uus-Sadama 23, tel: 6806 600, fax 6806 601, <www.tallinnhotels.ee>.* There's a decidedly hip, dynamic edge to the interior design and the service at Portus, but the real strengths of this 107-room hotel are the location, across from the passenger port's D-Terminal, and the huge number of extras for the price. These include a sauna, free internet terminals in the lobby and a children's playroom. There's also the rock-and-roll-themed Café Retro, where you can get pizzas, burgers and the like. Rooms are stylish with cork floors, satellite TV and wireless internet connection.

Domina Ilmarine €€ *Põhja pst. 23, tel: 6140 900, fax: 6140 901, <www.dominahotels.ee>.* A top-notch hotel cleverly built into a late 19th-century industrial complex. Forty-six of its 155 rooms are split-level. These surround an indoor atrium and have park or sea views and their own kitchenettes. All rooms are equipped with either wireless or fixed-line Internet connections, and computers can be requested. The hotel also offers meeting rooms, sauna, a restaurant, lounge and café.

Reval ExpressHotel € *Sadama 1, tel: 6678 700, fax: 6678 800, <www.revalhotels.com>.* Located just a few metres from Tallinn's main passenger port, the modern ExpressHotel caters mainly to ferry passengers looking for economy and convenience. It doesn't offer much in the way of extra services, but rooms are fully furnished and immaculately clean, service is very professional, and the café's well-known soup buffet is a true bargain. 166 rooms.

FURTHER AFIELD

Bridgettine Convent Guesthouse € *Merevälja tee 18, tel: 6055 000, fax: 6055 010, <www.osss.ee>.* The nuns of the Catholic Bridgettine Order operate this 20-room guesthouse in the Pirita beach district, 10–15 minutes' drive from the centre. The modern facility overlooks the fascinating ruins of the 15th-century Bridgettine Convent, often the site of classical concerts in summer. Each room is modern, comfortable and has its own shower and phone. TV and kitchen are shared. Cash only.

Dzingel € *Männiku tee 89, tel: 6105 201, fax: 6105 245, <www.dzingel.ee>.* This sprawling hotel in the pine-filled Nõmme district is popular with budget tourists who don't mind travelling the 6km (4 miles) to and from the city centre. While not as flashy as its more central rivals, the Dzingel offers a modern grill restaurant, saunas, conference rooms, an 'Internet corner' and spa treatments. Its 180 rooms are standard and more than adequate. There's a convenient bus connection.

Ecoland € *Randvere tee 115, tel: 6051 999, fax: 6051 998, <www.ecoland.ee>*. Old-fashioned designs, parrots, goldfish and an endless jumble of antiques create an almost storybook feel in this boutique hotel. Rooms have phone, cable-TV and showers with heated floors. Morning sauna and use of the swimming pool are included in the price. Restaurant, laundry and dry-cleaning services are also available. The hotel is 15–20 minutes by car from the centre. 76 rooms.

Tähetorni € *Tähetorni 16, tel. 6779 100, fax: 6779 110, <www. thotell.ee>*. From the outside Tähetorni has the appearance of a tiny castle, while the interior of this fairly new brick structure is a labyrinth of odd hallways and spiral staircases. Guests have a bar, sauna, conference rooms and a restaurant with an outside terrace at their disposal. Rooms are large and fully equipped. The hotel is 9km (6 miles) from the centre. 35 rooms.

Valge Villa € *Kännu 26/2, tel: 6551 196, fax: 6542 302, <www. white-villa.ee>*. This intimate, family-run guesthouse in the Kristiine suburb, 3km (2 miles) from the centre, is considered one of the best in its class. Most rooms are decorated in a comfortable, rustic style, and all have TV, refrigerator and Internet connections. Larger rooms have kitchens. Sauna, laundry facilities and bicycle hire are available. 10 rooms.

Viimsi Tervis SPA Hotel € *Randvere tee 11, Viimsi, tel: 6061 000, fax: 6061 003, <www.viimsitervis.ee>*. Health-conscious travellers will be interested in this relatively new resort on the Viimsi peninsula, 9km (6 miles) north of central Tallinn. In addition to 104 hotel-style rooms, the complex offers a large swimming pool, fitness centre, various saunas, beauty treatments, health treatments and even a plastic surgery clinic.

Recommended Restaurants

Visitors, like locals, usually end up in the Old Town, and where the crowds go, the restaurants follow. It's no surprise then that Tallinn's most interesting restaurants are concentrated here, reaching a critical mass on and around Town Hall Square. A large number of theme restaurants each try to outdo the next in terms of exotic cuisine and unusual ambience, to say nothing of bizarrely costumed waiters loitering outside.

Casual dress is fine for just about every kind of establishment, but for the higher-priced restaurants, 'smart casual' is the way to go.

Though you'll never have trouble finding a place to eat in the Old Town, the popular restaurants fill up quickly on weekends, so reservations are a good idea for Friday and Saturday night dining.

The price categories below are based on the average cost of a three-course meal for one person, and do not include drinks or tip. Restaurants take major credit cards except where noted, but keep in mind that American Express hasn't achieved 'major' status in Estonia.

€€€€	over 350kr
€€€	250–350kr
€€	150–250kr
€	under 150kr

OLD TOWN

African Kitchen €€ *Uus 34, tel: 6442 555.* The notion of a Tallinn restaurant specialising in African cuisine might seem bizarre at first, but once you arrive and sample the tasty main dishes, all doubts will be removed. African expatriates working in the kitchen ensure authenticity, and the intricate, vivid décor, particularly in the 'cave room', definitely makes this place worth a look.

Café Anglais €€ *Raekoja plats 14, upstairs, tel: 6442 160.* Set up like a classic, European café, this airy room overlooking Town Hall

Square is an easy choice for an informal meal. Tasty quiches, pastas and soups dominate the chalkboard menu. Salads come in two sizes, the larger of which could do as a main course. Excellent coffee and cakes.

Controvento €€–€€€ *Vene 12, tel: 6440 470.* Consistently high-quality Italian cuisine and professional service has made Controvento a long-time favourite of Tallinn's expatriate community. The setting, a cosy medieval building in the Katariina passageway, encourages people to linger for hours, ordering course after course from *bruschetta* to *tiramisu*. Reservations on weekends are essential.

Elevant €€€ *Vene 5, tel: 6313 132.* Considered the best of the Old Town's Indian restaurants, Elevant could easily win awards with its interior design alone. Everything from the iron staircase to the beautifully furnished dining rooms makes this a soothing escape from the tourist bustle outside. A long list of traditional curries, *biriyanis* and *masalas* is rounded out with a clever, Estonian-inspired 'wild menu' that features items such as moose *vindaloo* and wild boar mushroom *korma*.

Gloria €€€€ *Müürivahe 2, tel: 6446 950.* Gloria is the sort of restaurant people go to when they truly want to spoil themselves. The restaurant, which opened in 1937, has hosted a number of statesmen and dignitaries, including Pope John Paul II and Lech Walesa. The interior is a study in pre-war decadence – antiques, potted palms and private booths closed off by velvet curtains. An interesting mix of French, Italian, Baltic and Russian creations makes up the menu. Anyone who wants to taste a bit of Gloria's glory without committing to a full meal can visit its attractive wine cellar.

Golden Dragon €€ *Pikk 37, tel: 6313 506.* This cellar venue might look tired compared to the rash of flashier Chinese restaurants that have opened since the end of the 1990s, but Golden Dragon wins the race because of its consistently scrumptious food and great service. It can also be economical – portions of spring rolls are large enough to share, and the lunch special (served Mon–Fri noon–4pm) involves a soup, salad and main course for just 69kr. Rice is ordered separately.

Karja Kelder € *Väike-Karja 1, tel: 6441 008.* Cheap, filling Estonian pub food, the kind that would cause your cardiologist to faint, is the reason to seek out this popular cellar haunt. Hefty plates of grilled trout, pepper steak and schnitzel are washed down with mug after mug of beer. Karja Kelder gets crowded in the evenings so arrive early and be prepared to pay 6kr for the coat check.

Klafira €€€ *Vene 4, tel: 6675 144.* Furnished with extravagant, overstuffed antiques and staffed by waitresses in dazzling folk costumes, Klafira offers a highly stylised taste of pre-revolutionary Russia. Classic Russian dishes such as *pelmeni* and *borscht* are rounded out with more complex creations such as cutlet *à la Pozarski* and ox fillets with mushroom sauce. Live music and dancing nightly.

Kompressor € *Rataskaevu 3, tel: 6464 210.* More of a pub than a fully fledged restaurant, this popular student haunt is a budget traveller's dream. There are other items on the menu, but what draws the crowds to Kompressor are its enormous pancakes filled with things like smoked chicken, turkey, prawn and garlic cheese. One portion is a meal in itself and, at 30–45kr, a true bargain. Be prepared to wait.

Le Bonaparte €€€€ *Pikk 45, tel: 6464 444.* Fine, French cuisine in a beautifully restored, 17th-century merchant's house. Guests can opt for the formal dining in the main restaurant, visit the Cellar le Bonaparte downstairs for light meals and wine, or just drop into the foyer café for pastries and cakes. In all cases, a quality experience.

Maikrahv €€€–€€€€ *Raekoja plats 8, tel: 6314 227.* Named after the Count of May, a key figure in Tallinn's medieval spring festivals, this cellar restaurant on Town Hall Square presents carefully prepared international-style dishes in a very refined environment. The medieval décor makes it unique for restaurants of this class, and groups can order full medieval banquets.

Mõõkkala €€–€€€ *Kuninga 4, tel: 6418 288.* Mõõkkala (Swordfish) is both a fish-lover's paradise and a long-time Tallinn favourite. Perch, salmon, eel, crab, mussels and other delicacies of the sea, not to mention the restaurant's signature swordfish dish, are all expertly prepared and served with flair. The artistically decorated interior is equally captivating.

Moskva €€ *Vabaduse väljak 10, tel: 6404 694.* Moskva's small, ground-floor café-bar is nice enough, but head upstairs to immerse yourself in the ultra-cool air of the trendy restaurant. The menu is made up mainly of salads and light dishes as if catering to catwalk models, and of course this is a WiFi zone, so remember to bring your laptop.

Olde Hansa €€€ *Vana turg 1, tel: 6279 020.* This medieval-style restaurant in the heart of the Old Town may appear touristy from the outside, but once you dine here you'll understand why a visit to Tallinn wouldn't be complete without experiencing Olde Hansa. Far more intricate and authentic than a typical theme restaurant, it offers a fascinating menu and a truly Hanseatic atmosphere, complete with costumed waitresses, candlelight and minstrels. Reserve on weekends.

Pegasus €€€€ *Harju 1, tel: 6314 040.* Its sharp-looking interior and view of St Nicholas Church are certainly pluses, but what makes Pegasus famous is top-notch world cuisine prepared under the strict direction of an experienced London chef. The bar on the ground floor is considered one of Tallinn's most sophisticated places to mingle. Closes early on Sundays.

Pizza Americana € *Müürivahe 2, tel: 6448 837.* When looking to fill up on pizza in Tallinn it's hard to go wrong with Americana. It offers roughly 60 varieties of tasty, thick-crust pizza, all of which are served up still in the pan. Pizzas come in two sizes, the 'small' being large enough for one hungry person and costing around 100kr. Casual, colourful furnishings make this a friendly place for the kids. Americana will also deliver to your hotel.

Silk €€€ *Kullassepa 4, tel: 6484 625.* A long list of intriguing sushi choices, soups, tempura and other Japanese favourites are on the menu at Silk. The black interior gives this small restaurant a chic, cosmopolitan feel and the location near Town Hall Square makes it equally popular. For something different, try the green-tea-flavoured ice-cream.

Troika €€€ *Raekoja plats 15, tel: 6276 245.* Resembling something straight out of a 19th-century Russian storybook, this lavishly decorated cellar restaurant is not one you'll soon forget. The menu ranges from *blini* to Tver mutton and includes bear *stroganoff*. The Town Hall Square location makes Troika a busy place, so reserve a table.

Vana Tunnel €€–€€€ *Harju 6, tel: 6310 631.* One of the most unusual dining venues you'll find anywhere, Vana Tunnel (Old Tunnel) is built inside a long, underground passage that was constructed in the 14th-century as an aqueduct. Furnishings are otherwise modern and smart, and orders are brought to the table on a hot grill plate. Closed Sundays.

Vanaema Juures €€€ *Rataskaevu 10, tel: 6269 080.* Just as you might expect from a restaurant called Grandmother's Place, this quiet cellar venue is bursting with antiques and old photographs and has a friendly atmosphere. It's also Tallinn's cosiest Estonian restaurant and an excellent place to try national dishes. Closes early Sundays.

TOWN CENTRE AND KADRIORG

Admiral €€€ *Lootsi 15, tel: 6623 777.* Near the passenger port's D-Terminal you'll find this 1950s-era steamship that's been cleverly rebuilt into an elegant, romantic restaurant with a beautifully decorated interior. The menu is a wide-ranging mix that includes several Balkan specialities, including Serbian lamb dishes, and a few Russian favourites. Its summer deck, with views of the city, is open from May to September. Phone ahead to make sure it hasn't been hired for a cruise.

Cantina Carramba €€–€€€ *Weizenbergi 20a, tel: 6013 431.* Tallinn's most authentic Tex-Mex restaurant is a worthy choice for lunch when visiting the adjacent Kadriorg Park. The fun, pueblo-style interior is almost as alluring as the mouth-watering *quesadillas, fajitas* and *burritos* served here. The number of chillies next to each dish on the menu indicates the spice level.

Double Coffee €€ *Pärnu mn. 15, tel: 6679 120.* One of a growing number of trendy cafés catering to Tallinn's young, professional set, Double Coffee sets itself apart by offering a much wider food menu than most. Sandwiches, filled pancakes, and several kinds of sushi are all available, as are some fairly exotic teas and, as the name suggests, coffee.

Eesti Maja €€ *Lauteri 1, tel: 6455 252.* Specialising in Estonian national cuisine, this friendly, downtown restaurant is the best place in town to try local favourites such as Baltic sprats, *mulgikapsad* (sauerkraut stew) and *sült* (jellied pork). The casual, folksy atmosphere makes this a good choice for families.

Lydia €€€€ *Koidula 13a, tel: 6268 990.* A touch of the unabashedly bourgeois is presented in this elegant, 1930s-style restaurant in the leafy, upper-class Kadriorg district. Patrons can sip brandy by the fireplace or delve into the long (and pricey) menu of intriguing dishes like smoked salmon tagliatelle or ostrich paté. Closes early Sundays.

Restoran Kadriorg €€€–€€€€ *Weizenbergi 18, tel: 6013 636.* Catering to the demands of Kadriorg's young, professional elite, this relatively new restaurant is a modern and trendy alternative to typically traditional upmarket fare. One floor offers a short, European menu heavy on grill items, while another is a 'spaghetteria' where pasta is king. Closes early Sundays.

Stefanie's €€€ *Maakri 19/21, tel: 6612 612.* This smart, international-style restaurant adjacent to the Radisson Hotel strikes just the right balance between high-class charm and arty informality. It's no surprise then that Stefanie's has become a hit with the business lunch crowd. Drop by in the evening for a more subdued atmosphere and try the duck breast fillet with teriyaki or one of the excellent pastas.

Villa Thai €€–€€€ *Vilmsi 6, tel: 6419 347.* Spicy Thai delicacies and irresistible Indian (tandoori) specialities are equally available at this popular Kadriorg haunt. Management take extra care to ensure a soothing ambience, Buddha statue and indoor fountain included. Lunch specials are also available, served weekdays, noon–2.30pm.

Woodstock €–€€ *Tatari 6, tel: 6604 854.* Woodstock is a downmarket music bar but well worth visiting just to get a look at the funky, 1960s–70s décor – something resembling a psychedelic Beatles album cover. Among the simple, inexpensive food items are a pork dish called 'Killer Pig' and a chicken salad dubbed 'Atomic Rooster'.

FURTHER AFIELD

Galaxy €€ *Kloostrimetsa 58a, tel: 6238 250.* It is difficult to label the cuisine served in the TV Tower's restaurant – everything from Greek salad (around 50kr) to chicken Kiev (about 100kr) is on the menu. The décor is formal and the food is decent, but the real reason for dining here is the breathtaking view of nearby forests and harbours from the tower's 170-m (560-ft) observation deck. Bear in mind that you will have to purchase a 50kr entrance ticket to the tower.

Paat €€–€€€ *Rohuneeme tee 53, Viimsi, tel: 6090 840.* On the shore just north of Tallinn stands this unusual structure shaped like a gigantic, overturned boat. One floor is an elegant restaurant, the other is a popular pub, but Paat's real treasure is its beautiful, seaside terrace with views of Tallinn Bay – an unbeatable escape from the city crowds.

INDEX